For the Sake of the Children

To Vic and Vera, who simply loved their grandchildren

For the Sake of the Children

The FNF Guide to Shared Parenting

Revised and updated edition

Sue Secker

FAMILIES NEED FATHERS

FNF Publications

Copyright © Sue Secker & Families Need Fathers 2009
First published in 2001 by FNF Publications
Families Need Fathers, 134 Curtain Road, London EC2A 3AR
tel: 020 7613 5060 email: fnf@fnf.org.uk
Revised edition published 2009

British Library Cataloguing in Publication Data
A catalogue record for this book is available from the British Library.

ISBN 978-0-9539307-2-2

Cover design by Tony Denton, Wapple Creative, Shere, Surrey
Typeset by Amolibros, Milverton, Somerset
www.amolibros.com
This book production has been managed by Amolibros
Printed and bound by T J International Ltd, Padstow, Cornwall, UK

Dedication

Your children are not your children
They are the sons and daughters of Life's longing for itself.
They come through you but not from you,
And though they are with you yet they belong not to you.
You may give them your love but not your thoughts,
For they have their own thoughts.
You may house their bodies but not their souls
For their souls dwell in the house of tomorrow,
Which you cannot visit, not even in your dreams.
You may strive to be like them, but seek not to make them like you.
For life goes not backward, nor tarries with yesterday.

(An extract from *The Prophet* by Kahlil Gibran)

CONTENTS

ACKNOWLEDGEMENTS

Families Need Fathers (FNF) would like to thank all who contributed to this project, especially the following:

Funding: the guide was originally funded by the Home Office. The Department for Children, Schools and Families have funded the second edition. These valuable contributions to the charitable work of FNF are greatly appreciated.

Related Organisations: a range of organisations and charities that share similar concerns were contacted as part of the background research, including:

Gingerbread, Grandparents Federation (now Grandparents' Association), Mothers Apart from Their Children, National Council for One Parent Families (now merged with Gingerbread), National Stepfamily Association (now part of Parentline Plus), National Association of Child Contact Centres, Childline, the Family Court Welfare Service (now Cafcass).

Seminars: National Council for Family Proceedings and Family Policy Studies Centre seminars provided helpful insights into the views of professionals and academics working with families. Sadly, these two forward-looking organisations have ceased to be.

FNF members and their families made the most valuable contribution to this project. The guide would not have been possible without their generous responses to requests for information or advice.

Critical readers (members of FNF and others) volunteered to read various drafts of the guide. Their constructive comments undoubtedly shaped and improved the final version.

Research support: Dr Ian Buchanan, University College, Northampton.

Main project managers: FNF Trustees, past and present.

The guide was researched and compiled for FNF by Sue Secker MA.

Special thanks to Dodie Masterman and Oceana Masterman-Smith for their illustrations.

Extract from *The Prophet* by Kahlil Gibran reproduced by kind permission of the Gibran National Committee, PO Box 116-52375, Beirut, Lebanon.

AUTHOR'S NOTE

This second edition of *For the Sake of the Children* has been updated to reflect changes to policy and practices that impact on separated families. Since 2001, some aspects of the law relating to our families have moved forward. It is also encouraging to see that government guidance to those working with separated families is beginning to reflect the importance for children of the continuing support of their 'whole' family, especially fathers.

But the assumptions and attitudes about arrangements for children when parents live apart are slower to change. Despite all the progress towards equality, separated parents are treated differently, because it is still commonplace to assume that children will 'live' with one parent (almost always the mother).

For example, the system still hasn't adapted to the fact that care and responsibility for children can be shared by both parents: it's not yet geared to dividing state benefits between children's homes (plural).

This impacts upon the allocation of Children's Tax Credits, eligibility for housing (but see p36), and calculations for child maintenance. Irrationally, even where there is a Shared Residence Order in place (p90), only one parent is expected to pass money to the other, even if children spend considerable amounts of time with both parents. Regrettably, prescriptive terminology also labels only one parent as the 'parent with care'.

And as yet, family support is still not geared to fathers having to live apart from their children. So much more could and should be done to show that the continuing involvement of both parents is valuable and valued...a key, liberating message for children.

But change, especially the impact upon culture, takes a while to filter through...and as it has done for over thirty-five years, FNF will be watching carefully to assess whether legal and policy changes bring the results that separated families, especially children, deserve.

So in a nutshell, we're not out of the woods yet...and guides like this, that reflect the day-to-day reality of life for the overlooked and undervalued half of a child's family, are still essential reading and preparation, preferably before the shock of separation from children hits home.

This guide aims to provide a basic, jargon-busting overview of 'separation' for those possibly on the brink of losing a continuing, full, loving relationship with their children.

Anyone working with families throughout separation will also gain insights into the reality of life for fathers (or mothers) who choose to be anything but 'absent'. This will help to encourage greater support for both parents to play a meaningful part in their children's lives.

We hope that this guide may also give food for thought to *both* parents, for the sake of their children.

WHAT IS FAMILIES NEED FATHERS?

Founded in 1974, Families Need Fathers (FNF) is a national charity dedicated to 'Keeping Children and Parents in Contact'. The mission of FNF is to help children, by helping their parents (and grandparents, etc.) to stay involved with their family after divorce or separation. The charity is delighted that the Department for Children, Schools and Families (DCSF) was able to fund the second edition of this guide[1] for those trying to support children through a difficult and often bewildering experience.

FNF is the main provider of both practical and emotional support for parents apart from children. Every year, the charity meets the needs of many thousands of parents who seek sympathetic, practical support during the confusing and stressful experience of divorce or separation. Some members remain active in FNF long after their own family problems have been resolved, providing encouragement and support to newer members.

Volunteer-led support is provided through a network of local contacts, evening branch meetings, Internet discussion groups, and day workshops. A National Telephone Helpline supports thousands of callers each year. FNF also publishes *McKenzie*, a regular newsletter, and a range of leaflets and booklets. Further information can be found on FNF's comprehensive website: **www.fnf.org.uk**

FNF promotes shared parenting and equality after divorce or separation. It campaigns to raise awareness of the consequences for children when they lose contact with one of their parents (usually, but not always the father). It supports the use of family mediation to reduce conflict and potential harm to the children. Until policies and practices concerned with family breakdown reinforce the right of children to benefit from the care and involvement of both parents, there will continue to be a need for FNF.

---

1   Although this publication has been funded by the DCSF, it has been prepared by Families Need Fathers. The views expressed in this document are not necessarily those of the government.

"Men have always had problems discussing their feelings. A show of emotion is considered unmanly, yet there is not one father in FNF who has not secretly cried about the loss of his children. Putting those tears on paper would produce more results than all the lawyers in the kingdom."

(Stan Hayward 1999)

This guide draws on the experiences of FNF members past and present in order *to help parents make their own positive and realistic decisions about their family situation*. Wherever possible, original contributions and quotations have been included, but personal details have been changed to protect the identities of families.

The advice offered is practical rather than idealistic: families have to face the world as it is now, not as it could be. It will be of interest to anyone who wants to reduce conflict and increase support for children when parents live apart.

FOREWORD

Dr Hamish Cameron FRCP FRCPsych DPM
Consultant Child Psychiatrist, and Patron of FNF

The publication of a second edition of *For the Sake of the Children* might lead readers to conclude merely that old ground needs working over more thoroughly. That would be to overlook the steady progress of the past decade, for this book's reappearance in updated form is both a celebration of small steps already taken, and an indication of work yet to be done.

If a child is to develop into the person he or she wishes to be, we need to look at the world through their eyes. Children flourish when comfortably at ease with both sides of their family; while a child, living with just one parent, often has to stifle their longing for their other parent.

These days, not before time, professional debate tends to be less adult-focused, and more child-centred. It is now widely accepted that young adults' conduct crucially derives from the parenting and affection that they received in childhood. Research findings suggest that this country's children are not as high a priority as we might like to think, for the statistics place us woefully low in league tables. The pivotal issue is how to keep each child's development on the right track. This requires more than 'supporting marriage' or supporting 'family life', laudable though these aims are. For at the heart of a good childhood upbringing lies both parents' shared parental responsibility.

For generations Parliament reflected society's underlying indifference to children's welfare, especially in the matter of parental divorce and separation. The authorities were slow to accept their neglect of these children. But recent moves towards reform should begin to protect more children from the harmful impact of family breakdown on their immature personalities. In the past, the breakdown of adult relationships was seen as a private matter even when children were involved. But these days the benefits of sustaining family ties are increasingly on the public agenda, as are joined-up parenting-guidance and conciliation remedies monitored by the court.

The Family Courts, taking their cue from society and the media, sometimes used to value a grown-up's plans for their own happiness above their child's need for both parents. Such an approach ignores the fact that while adults can decide to partner, it's a choice that may also be undone. But children just take it for granted that they have both their parents for life. At present, separating parents become either a co-parenting family apart, that makes the best of it, or non-co-operators, to the detriment of their child. In the future separating parents are likely to be told at the earliest opportunity what the court expects from them, and what outcome, in broad terms, the court is contemplating for their child.

Children hate being argued over as a possession, and just want their separating parents to agree a plan that is good for all the family. A child's love for each parent continues; they don't want to choose one parent over the other. And, of course, all children should be included fully in both parents' extended families, especially with their grandparents, and not be burdened or overpowered by one parent undermining the other.

Good parenting has been the aim for years. The target nowadays is a good childhood. In his Father's Day message, President Barack Obama, who understands the importance of fatherhood through its absence in his own childhood and in the lives of others, signals the qualities we should nourish in our children – gentleness and trust, a capacity for affection, and an appetite for learning. Parents can reach closer to producing this good childhood if they absorb the wise guidance of this creative, detailed and practical book rooted in the human realities of post-separation family life.

Hamish Cameron.

Dr Hamish Cameron
Autumn 2009

Dr Hamish Cameron is a children's doctor, a child psychiatrist with many years' experience of giving evidence on behalf of children in the Family Courts. His unwavering conviction is that secure parenting by both parents and their families, pre- and post-separation, is optimal for children's well-being as they grow up. He has spoken at FNF's seminars, and has lectured to judicial conferences nationally for many years. He commends FNF's work and he feels privileged to have been chosen as one of its patrons.

Introduction

THE NEED FOR INFORMATION, ADVICE, SUPPORT

Being apart from dearly loved children is indescribably painful, for mothers *and* fathers. It is also deeply upsetting for other relations, grandparents, uncles, aunts, etc. who have known and loved the children. Separation from a loved and loving family is distressing and damaging for children.

The sense of loss can be overwhelming. Men may find it difficult to show they are suffering emotionally. Nevertheless, they are just as hurt, and in need of support.

Parents (mainly fathers) contact FNF because they want to continue to play a meaningful part in their children's upbringing. Many will be having difficulty negotiating time with their children either with the other parent or via a court agreement. Some will have little or no parenting time at all, despite being willing and able to be more involved.

Grandparents and members of the wider family contact FNF for the same reason. They also suffer the consequences of less or lost time with children who once were part of their lives. It is difficult for them to imagine why children should not continue to benefit from these special family relationships. Many new partners also seek advice because they recognise the distress to their partners and children and don't know how best to help.

An added pressure is that those caught in this situation may have difficulty discussing these issues in case it makes matters worse for their family. If they are in the middle of court proceedings they are legally bound not to disclose certain information that might identify children. Anything that could be judged negatively is likely to influence the court's decision.

It is difficult to remain calm and focused when the whole process is unintelligible, seems to drag on for ages, with the risk that the slightest show of emotion might be misjudged and count against you.

> **Finding that the relationship you once had with your children is slipping away**
>
> **That there appears to be little you can do to stop it happening**
>
> **No service to whom you can turn for support and advice**
>
> **No one who is able to prevent this happening**
>
> **IS AN ISOLATING AND DEEPLY STRESSFUL EXPERIENCE.**

There is little empathy with parents, usually fathers, who find this happening to their family. They are mainly seen as unable to come to terms with a situation judged as inevitable. They need advice, information and guidance on how best to cope with the frustration and powerlessness. They especially need sympathetic support. Some can find all this and more by making contact with FNF, perhaps at an FNF local branch meeting. Discovering that others are 'in the same boat' can be a lifeline. There are many reasons why it may not be possible to get to a meeting. And there are those that cannot, or choose not to, seek support but who still need that lifeline.

Don't give up hope

This guide is based on the firsthand experiences of many members of FNF and their families, past and present. The one clear message that comes across is: *'**Don't give up hope.'**** Everyone who understands the ache of separation from children either firsthand or having watched someone close to them suffering has said the same thing.

Things may improve: eventually children who perhaps believed that Dad (or Mum) didn't care or worse, had abandoned them, might begin to realise they were loved after all. It happens all the time. Hopefully this will strengthen your own natural desire to be involved with your children, and encourage you not to give up on this even when it becomes difficult.

> ➢ *You are right to want to be there for them.*
> ➢ *Don't feel guilty.*
> ➢ *Don't let anyone persuade you that you are wrong.*
> ➢ *It is absolutely natural to love your children.*
> ➢ *It is their right to know that you do.*

That's the easy bit: dealing with all the complex and stressful surrounding issues is not so easy.

> *No one knows what lies ahead when their*
> *family splits up. You will need all the help*
> *available to make sense of what is happening*
> *as soon as possible. Mistakes made early on*
> *may set the pattern for all that is to follow,*
> *and if not managed positively can seriously*
> *affect the prospects for a continuing*
> *relationship with children.*

It is often only looking back that we recognise where things went wrong, the mistakes we made with good intentions at the time. This could be due to lack of information, not understanding 'the system' and also to making assumptions about what should or could happen next.

Parts One and Two of this guide offer practical advice on how best to cope positively with the many changes and situations that you may have to face.

Part Three includes a brief overview of the law relating to families, and the people who might become involved as you try to sort out the next part of your parenting life.

Part Four is a reference section and includes other sources of information, and suggestions for further reading.

The ultimate aim in the short and long-term, is to help you maintain the best relationship possible with your children, whatever the circumstances.

Limitations of the guide

> ➤ *The guide is not a panacea: you will not find magic answers or quick-fix solutions.*
> ➤ *It cannot change reality: you must deal with what has to be faced now.*
> ➤ *It cannot change attitudes overnight.*

➢ *It cannot offer a blueprint for any specific family situation, or individual: the vast differences between families and individuals make this impossible.*

A word of caution about taking advice

Advice from professionals you may meet or even other FNF members, is often phrased so authoritatively, that it appears as if it is the only course of action open. It can be very persuasive, but there may well be other alternatives, ones perhaps more suitable for you and your family. Bear in mind that this advice may be based on *opinions,* albeit opinions born out of professional or personal experience. Some members of FNF have special expertise and considerable experience: others may best offer support and sympathy. Always seek more than one opinion, preferably a wide range, then make a decision based on what suits you and your family situation. If you feel uncomfortable with whatever is suggested, it may not be right for you. Only you can weigh up the personalities involved, how people might react.

☛ Always consider the impact upon your children. ☛

Basic principles

Although there can never be a solution or plan of action that suits every individual or set of circumstances, there does appear to be a consensus about the best way to proceed if you are able to do so.

➢ Children should be free to receive the maximum support from the widest possible family network, *especially* when the relationship between their parents has broken down.

➢ Both parents should encourage this support.

➢ *Do try* to work out informal agreements regarding arrangements for children with the other parent.

➢ *Don't* assume you will not be able to do this.

➢ *Do take action quickly* if all attempts to reach agreement fail, and your children are losing contact with you.

➢ *Don't* assume it is in their interests to 'give up' for whatever reason.

The guide is therefore based on these simple child-centred principles. In many respects, it will suggest how you can make the best of situations that should not exist in the first place. *You are not on your own.* FNF has a long history of supporting families as they try to make sense of life after divorce or relationship breakdown. Most eventually sort out their problems.

☛ *Don't ever give up hope.* ☛

SETTING THE SCENE

It has been estimated that around two in five children will have experienced the breakdown of their parents' relationship by the time they reach sixteen. The average length of a relationship before it falters is around seven years, therefore many children will be very young when their parents part. The majority will subsequently live with just one parent for a while. In 2004, around twenty-five per cent of all dependent children were living in lone-parent households. The ratio of lone mothers to lone fathers was 22:2 (*Dependent Children, 2005*, Office for National Statistics: Part Four, No 47). Note: there were no statistics showing whether overall care of children was shared between both parents.

Children are vulnerable when their parents separate, and any arrangement for their lives must be sensitive to their needs. Some families will be able to sort out arrangements amicably, but many seek court orders because they are unable to resolve problems. In 2007-2008 there were more than 39,000 'private' (see p90) family law applications. These applications are not only made at the time of separation but also when problems arise, sometimes years afterwards.

This may be the tip of the iceberg: many thousands of families contact FNF every year. There must be others needing help who may not realise that they could get specialist advice, etc. from experienced organisations such as FNF. Men often feel they should be able to cope on their own. They may be afraid to ask, not know whom to ask. Many will not have considered they might ever need help, until they realise they may be about to lose their children.

This middle ground also includes those who have not really resolved the breakdown of their family in the best way possible for children. Some are simply too hurt, or have just accepted they cannot see their children. They may have decided the legal route is not for them. They may not be able to afford the legal costs, or not want to involve their children in a 'battle'.

The percentage of fathers who lose contact with children is quoted, but it is seldom acknowledged that this may not be their choice. The fathers who join

FNF are not part of these 'lost father statistics'. They are often parents living apart from children, who in many cases did not have any say in the breakdown of their family, who undoubtedly want to continue to be responsible parents. They cannot understand why their input is not properly recognised. They miss being involved, part of their children's lives.

They speak of no longer being able to help with everyday things like reading bedtime stories, playing football at the park, or with homework. They may not have any input into major decisions like choice of schools, etc. Frankly, they miss just 'being there' for their children.

The other parent may be resisting their involvement, perhaps not co-operating over arrangements, or may have refused to allow any contact at all. That they are able to do this reflects the greater power they assume they have to make decisions for children. Mums or dads living apart from children can experience the same exclusion, and be relatively powerless.

FNF has played a major role in raising awareness of the valuable contribution that each parent can and should make especially after family breakdown. Attitudes in society *are* beginning to change, and there is increasing recognition of the benefits to children when both parents can be involved in their upbringing.

Unmarried fathers and 'Parental Responsibility'

The Children Act 1989 introduced the concept of Parental Responsibility (PR). All mothers and all married fathers automatically have PR for their children, but the situation is different for some unmarried fathers (see Court Orders concerning children, p90).

Prior to 1st Dec 2003, unmarried fathers had no legal rights whatsoever in relation to their children unless they had made a legally binding agreement with the mother or obtained a court order. Having their name on the child's birth certificate or paying child support gave them no legal rights.

From 1st Dec 2003, unmarried fathers now have PR automatically if they have registered the birth of a child jointly with the child's mother. But this legislation is not retrospective and therefore does not apply to births registered before that date.

Unmarried fathers whose names are not shown on birth certificates and whose children's births were registered prior to 1st December 2003 can re-register the birth jointly with the mother to obtain PR. However, if a father's name is already on a child's birth certificate, he cannot re-register and therefore cannot obtain PR by this method.

Unmarried fathers can acquire Parental Responsibility for their children by making a Parental Responsibility Agreement with the mother on a standard form (one for each child). The simplest way to do this is for both parents to go to the local court office together, taking along the required documentation. There is no fee and no need to go before a judge. Both parents must sign the form in the presence of an authorised official and lodge the agreement at the Principal Registry of the Family Division. Alternatively, the agreement can be made before any commissioner for oaths (but not your own solicitor), for a standard fee. Informal agreements, i.e. not registered as above, have no legal status.

If the mother will not agree, the father can apply to court for a Parental Responsibility Order (PRO). Few fathers are refused PR by the courts. An appeal against a refusal is usually successful. FNF produces an information sheet with detailed advice about drawing up an agreement and making a successful application for PR. The FNF website includes comprehensive and up-to-date information about PR.

Adding the father's name to the birth certificate

If a father's name is not on the birth certificate and he has parental responsibility then he can, even without the mother's consent, have the child's birth re-registered to include his name. There is no charge for this but, as with copies of all birth certificates, those containing the newly added information have to be paid for (more information on the General Record Office website: Part Four, No 42).

NB: It is being proposed that both parents' names must be on a child's birth certificate. Contact FNF for current information.

The significance of PR

The significance of PR is often not appreciated until it is too late, when the relationship between parents has broken down and decisions about children need to be made. If the father does not have PR, only the mother has the right to make decisions concerning children, from giving consent for an emergency operation, to whether they can be taken abroad on holiday, or even permanently. A mother could also sign a Parental Responsibility Agreement with her new husband, without needing the father's agreement. The stepfather would then have PR whilst the father would not. The father has no right to a legal role (except to provide child support), even if the children are put up for adoption. The father can, however, make application to the court in relation to these and other matters (either with or without the court's permission).

Services dealing with adoption have a duty to make reasonable enquiries about *both birth parents* when they are preparing their report for the court. Unmarried fathers without PR should be given the opportunity to express their wishes. The court should take these into account if they have had a relationship with their children at any time. There is insufficient time and limited funding available for extensive searches. Inevitably some fathers may not be 'found', and others learn of the imminent adoption too late to make any difference to the decision (also see Holidays overseas, p38 and Change of name, p63).

Always bear in mind that the reaction to legal action may be increased hostility (so timing may be crucial), but it is essential for your continuing involvement in your children's lives that you acquire PR. In many cases the mother will agree before the case gets to court.

Mediation

"Mediation helps couples to turn an argument into a negotiation."
(Thelma Fisher, National Family Mediation, 1997)

A contested court case is something that all parents should avoid if at all possible.

It is important for separating parents to consider using mediation to reduce any potential conflict for children. Unresolved conflict can affect relationships for years. If there is any residual goodwill between parents, mediation provides a real opportunity to reduce problems for the children. Some mediation services are publicly funded; others may charge a fee but successful use of mediation is likely to save money.

Note: The aim of mediation is not to get you back together with the other parent. From Relate's website:

"Mediation is not like counselling. It helps couples who have decided to separate or divorce with the practical aspects of a relationship break-up, like finance, property and parenting issues, and helps you come to an agreement over what should be done."

Mediation is a means of helping separating couples to make their own arrangements for the future with the help of an impartial third party. The main aim is to reduce unnecessary conflict by helping you and your family to get a better grasp of the issues that will have to be dealt with. You will be encouraged to explore common ground in the hope that you can reach an agreement. Where this is successful then a 'Parenting Plan' – a document agreed by the parents – may be suggested. This is likely to include a statement that the parents will work together in the children's interests, giving details of arrangements for holidays, schooling, medical treatment and other areas of potential dispute. Courts and those who work with separating families have also been directed to recommend parents to consider drawing up parenting plans early in any legal proceedings.

Parenting Plans

Further information on Parenting Plans is available from the Stationery Office (Part Four, No 79), from county courts and magistrates' courts dealing with family matters, solicitors' offices, mediation services, Cafcass offices or its website, and many voluntary organisations working directly with children. The FNF website includes examples of how parenting time can be shared more flexibly than the 'every other weekend and half the school holidays' model, *reflecting the needs of individual children and the circumstances of each parent*. It's also worth searching the websites of USA family courts (each State will be different: p41). Many have detailed information on sharing care according to ages and maturity of children (Part Four, Nos 64, 72 & 81).

Many parents who try the mediation process reach agreement. Even if you cannot agree, you might still reach some common ground. It also shows you are willing to co-operate. Remember that the court will want to see evidence that both parents have done all they can to try to resolve matters themselves. It is worth mentioning that what happens during mediation is usually confidential, and cannot be used to support any claims in court (unless a child is thought to be at risk).

There are two main national mediation organisations: the Family Mediators Association and National Family Mediation (Part Four, Nos 11 & 21). However, mediation services can be run by a variety of agencies, including solicitors. The service provided rests largely with the individuals running your session/s. They come from different backgrounds, ranging from psychoanalysts to lawyers. Views and practices can vary widely. If you are uncertain or don't understand something, ask for more information. It makes sense to go with an open mind. If all co-operate there is a real opportunity to work through contentious issues, mindful of the impact upon your children. Don't be afraid or embarrassed to give this a try. It may reduce the problems for your children, which is after all the main concern.

Experience suggests that 'out of court' mediation is preferable to 'in court' services. Cafcass (Children and Family Court Advisory Support Service, the service that will become involved if you do apply to court: see p101) is increasingly working with parents at the earliest opportunity to try to assist them reaching an agreement before a court hearing. It makes sense to take this opportunity to work through any areas of disagreement. But if you (and the other parent) feel under pressure to agree, don't let yourself be brow-beaten into something that you feel will not work, or is much less than your children need.

If you have applied for a court order perhaps because your children are not able to see you or your family, then subsequently you appear to have come to an agreement with the other parent, the court can be asked to turn this into an order. Only court orders have any legal standing. It might be worth suggesting that any mediated agreement is turned into a 'Consent Order'. Otherwise you may find that once the hearing is over, there is nothing to deter further resistance. This could mean yet another costly and stressful return to court, not to mention more disruption to your children's relationship with you. Be prepared to make a statement outlining your concerns, giving reasons why what's proposed might not ultimately be in their interests.

When there is disagreement about the way forward, how can conflict be reduced, and what could make it easier for children to benefit from the support of both parents?

Start from shared parenting principles

Decisions made early on, or the assumptions upon which these decisions are based, may set the pattern for much that is to come. For example, when parents separate, it is widely assumed that children will remain with mother. It is fair to say that mothers also presume that this will happen. They seldom question this outcome: *neither do fathers.*

"She has all the rights to the children."

Don't assume you must just accept a minor role in their lives. If you have PR (p8) you both have an equal right to take responsibility for your children when they are with you. And if you do not have PR, you will probably be able to obtain it. Fathers without PR can make application to the court in order to protect the interests of the child or resolve an issue concerning that child.

The rise in applications for court orders concerning children has been put down to fathers now 'exercising their newly found rights'. There may be an element of truth in that, because information is becoming more readily available.

However, it may really be more to do with fathers beginning to question the presumption that children are 'best left' with mother. They may apply for an order when they discover they are being excluded from their children's lives. Other legislation may actually be encouraging this exclusion (Child Support Act, p72). Children should be able to benefit from the best of both parents' worlds. In 2007, research by the Equal Opportunities Commission found that there has been a marked societal shift in the last twenty years; fathers nowadays report almost equal amounts of care as do mothers.

In reality, either parent can raise children. The debate about which parent is a better carer is largely irrelevant, especially when considering the long-term benefits of having a relationship with both parents. Each parent has their own qualities, strengths and weaknesses and children need them both, warts and all (Caring for children, p47). So, the advice must be, when deciding on arrangements for children, try to work towards a plan that will involve sharing the care and upbringing, rather than assuming one parent will 'get' the children, the other be relegated to the second parenting division. If the other parent seems reluctant to consider this, focus on the advantages for everyone if care is shared. If at all possible, try to reach agreement rather than go down the costly, conflict-ridden and unpredictable court route.

How you share the care will depend on your circumstances, e.g. the distance between the two parents' homes, your work patterns, etc. It may not be possible to divide parenting time equally, but the key factor is that both parents should be involved in decisions, rather than one assuming total responsibility. Crucially, children need to understand that they can still be part of each parent's life, and be encouraged to do so. *This does rely on both parents recognising that this is important for children.* Some children move freely between parents living in different countries. Others are not able or allowed to visit parents and wider family living just around the corner.

An uneven playing field

"The parent apart, but particularly a father, he must understand the playing field is not level and he is at the bottom of the field."

13

Many would say that legislation concerning children (Children Act 1989, p90) laid out a level parenting playing field. It is how the game has since evolved that places one parent at a disadvantage. The following is from the Children Act 1989 Guidance and Regulations:

> "A shared care order has the advantage of being more realistic in those cases where the child is to spend considerable amounts of time with both parents...and removes any impression that one parent is good and responsible whereas the other parent is not."

Shared Residence Orders (SROs, p90) can be made, not only when parents are able to co-operate, but crucially, when one parent will not encourage the involvement of the other parent. This reinforces and protects a child's right to have the love and support of both parents. Although SROs are quite commonly made by courts, many working with families may still not be fully aware (or supportive) of this child-focused option.

The precedent set if only one parent is treated as important may be difficult to reverse. Family services and professionals are more likely to work with the 'resident' parent and may overlook the one that lives elsewhere. You may find that it is not only the other parent, but also other professionals who become involved, that will need persuading re the benefits of sharing care more equally. You may have to challenge what they consider 'reasonable contact', a vague and undefined phrase that can lead to confusion and conflict. Also, the conditions imposed may be unnatural and unworkable. It is up to you to argue for a better outcome, for the sake of your children. Try to set a workable pattern immediately you and the other parent part (Accommodation, p35). Whatever routine develops can soon become the 'status quo'. Even if this means you are not seeing the children at all, the system is reluctant to disturb what is regarded as a working arrangement. Recent research shows this may not be taking children's wishes or needs fully into account.

> "You are doing the right thing: shared care is not unusual – it can and does work. PS. Thanks for the notification of the AGM. I shall not be able to attend because it is my week to look after the children."

Don't be put off by advice that it is more 'normal' for the children to live with one parent. It is far more normal to live with, or at least be able to be loved and supported by, a much wider network of people. But it is not all doom and gloom – increasingly we hear that judges are granting shared residence, in some instances, despite objections made by parents hostile to this outcome.

A Shared Residence Order stipulates that the child lives with *both* parents. Many fathers are now asking for these orders.

If you don't ask for shared residency, you are unlikely to get it, but remember to prepare your argument carefully, based on the advantages for your child.

NB: Cafcass (p101) may now be taking on board the importance for children to regard themselves as living in two homes, rather than having one home, and just 'visiting' one of their parents for 'contact' (p15). This is a fundamental, empowering message for children, regardless of whether there is a Shared Residence Order in place.

Realistically, given current attitudes, you may not achieve as much involvement as your children should have. How then, can you best help them, especially if they live somewhere else? If you desperately want to be a parent after family breakdown, but are forced to play a minor role, or have no input at all, you will not need to be told you should 'get involved'. **It is more a question of how *can* you get involved**. You may have relatively little or no choice about when, where or even if you see your children.

What is 'contact'?

Throughout this book, the word 'contact' occurs frequently. Throughout separation, you will also find 'contact' used in a range of contexts.

Sometimes its use is unavoidable: one of the Children Act 1989 court orders concerning children is a 'Contact Order'. Before 1989, the terms included in family law to describe division of parenting time with children, were 'custody' (and joint custody) and 'access'. When the law relating to children changed in 1989, the terms 'residence' (and shared residence) and 'contact' replaced and changed the original terms and what they represented (the old terms are still often used in media reports).

Sometimes using 'contact' is commonplace, as in: 'keeping in contact with', 'not being able to make contact with', or 'making contact with'. (Note: all these phrases imply that some form of distance precedes contact.)

The dilemma starts when 'contact' is used not just in the context of keeping children 'in contact' with their families throughout separation, but to symbolise what should be the ongoing relationship between a child and one of its parents, as in: "He is 'having contact' with his daughter." This has become shorthand for what is far broader and more fundamental to a child's life than just 'contact'. Think about it: before parents live apart, how often does either parent say, "I'm having contact with my child"? Isn't it more usual to say something like: "The children are spending time with dad/mum (or their grandparents) this weekend"?

But it seems that throughout separation, the term 'contact' becomes part of common culture, effectively pigeon-holing parents into one of two roles post-separation; 'resident' parent, with whom the child 'lives', and 'contact' parent, who visits or is visited.

Many seem to think that this is 'the law', and accept their parenting lot. But this does not reflect the Children Act principle that children should have a continuing 'relationship' with both their parents wherever possible (not just 'contact' for an hour or two every other weekend).

It's worth analysing whether being drawn into using this unhelpful term will achieve a shared parenting outcome for your child. Using 'contact' may simply perpetuate an artificial world post-separation, reinforcing the message that one parent is less important than the other, a 'fact' that children will also absorb, without realising that this is a limited outcome, and they have more options.

Far better to use more even-handed language and to aim for what children should be free to have, rather than what they commonly accept they are allowed. Think about it:

> *Do you wish the relationship between you and your child to be described as 'contact'?*

> *Do you wish to be known as the 'contact' parent?*

And do you wish your child to regard you as their 'contact' parent?

So if for example, the other parent, your solicitor, or a Cafcass officer (p102) is discussing 'contact' arrangements, take time to use language that will reflect the optimum result for your child, i.e. being able to spend time with both parents and wider family, not just 'having contact'.

> *Wherever possible, substitute the term 'parenting time', for 'contact'.*

> *Work from the premise that parenting time will be shared.*

For example, you could say: "Our children will need to spend time with both parents. Drawing up a Parenting Plan (p11) will establish how and when each of us will be 'on-duty'." (See p112.)

Making these small but significant changes can highlight the fact that children deserve far more than mere 'contact'.

The next section deals with the whole question of how to manage life as a parent in often frustrating and difficult circumstances. The first part focuses on how everything impacts upon children. At the end of the day, if you cannot change how the other parent or the courts have organised your role, your children are stuck with the consequences too. There may be little you can do to change attitudes or behaviour. You and your children will therefore have to make the best of what you have.

PART ONE: Being positive

WHAT *IS* BEST FOR CHILDREN?

Bringing up children is a demanding but rewarding job, made even more difficult by family breakdown. As all are making decisions for *your* family, the most repeated phrase you will hear is: *'Ah, but we have to consider the best interests of the child.'* All will think they know what's best. All too often, children will not be asked for *their* views, but, wherever possible they should be included in decisions that affect them. In fact, there *is* no one answer, but the guiding principle must be that it is best for them if they continue to benefit from their relationship with both parents and wider family support network.

What would they choose?

Undoubtedly, children, if free to choose, want both their parents, preferably back together again. If this is not possible, then the best compromise is to be able to be loved and cared for by both, parenting business as usual if from separate bases. They do not want to be asked to choose between parents, and they should not be given the ultimate responsibility for decisions about their lives, especially if their expectations cannot in reality be met. They inevitably love both their parents, regardless. The distress that children of all ages may suffer, as they become aware that their parents no longer want to stay together, is well documented.

> "I used to tell lies a lot, to try and make people believe I was leading a happy life."

The need to be included

A recent study of what children wanted in terms of support services at such times showed that they may feel isolated from events and decisions that will deeply affect their futures. They wanted to know what was happening, to be able to get information easily and informally. *The crucial thing to remember is that they should not be left out.* When parents are preoccupied with their own problems, coping with all the emotional turmoil, it is so easy to overlook the fact that children need help too. It's also hard to find appropriate help.

Even though their parents have decided not to live together, children need to know that the decision is based on the failure of that relationship, and is not because of them. When their lives are unsettled, they need extra reassurance that they are still loved by both parents. They can also feel that they are somehow responsible for what is happening: *'What did I do to make Dad (or Mum) leave?'* Make sure they don't blame themselves as they commonly will. It is also damaging if they mistakenly think that one parent is leaving *them,* or is solely responsible for the break-up of the family.

Children can feel largely powerless as parents and other adults re-shape their futures, as is obvious from this child's comments:

> "It was very stressful: you can't do it right. Everything was dictated – I had no choice. I couldn't say anything to anyone because I was afraid it would make it worse."

If they feel they are being considered, whatever has to happen next, there is a greater chance of coping with the inevitable compromises that will have to follow for everyone. *Why Are My Parents Separating?* is a story tape and booklet that parents might find useful to involve and support young children as their family changes (Part Four, No 86). Also see 'Putting yourself in your children's shoes', p110.

Conflicts of interest

As said earlier, there are many views about what's best for children, and many areas where there is disagreement even amongst 'experts'. The other thing that is not fully appreciated is that 'family life' after parents move apart is so very different to how it was before, when there was 'one base'. The same values and ideas about what is best for children cannot apply, need to be re-worked to take account of the restructure.

Despite different assumptions about what children need, there is both evidence and agreement that children suffer from the effects of conflict. All agree that conflict needs to be minimised. Separating one family unit into two is inevitably stressful. Not only are the financial problems immense, but there may also be resentment and/or an unwillingness to co-operate. As lives diverge, take on new identities, there may be even more conflicts of interests (New partners, p77, Maintenance, p69).

It is perhaps negative to assume that change in itself is the cause of problems, or that children cannot deal with change, must be protected from it. It is the way such changes are managed, how they are helped to cope with changes that is the crucial factor in how well they adapt. *Children are more flexible than is generally realised, and can survive best, if a constructive example is set for them.* Even when there are major areas of disagreement between parents, respect for the other's part in their life is essential if they are not to suffer deep, often long-term emotional damage.

Adapting to changes

For many children, the attempt to maintain a relationship with both parents after family breakdown is fraught with conflict. Many feel pressured to 'choose' between their parents, and suffer guilt because they may have to do so. One researcher described how children attempt to 'pare down their families' in order to cope with the competing demands. It is tragic for everyone, but especially the children, if they are effectively forced to reject part of their family.

Children learn to conform to the rules and cultural system in their original family. When there are two homes, there may be two sets of rules. Yet parents with international marriages report that children find it surprisingly easy to become bilingual and bicultural: *'Two homes are a cinch!'* It can have advantages, helping to broaden their understanding, making them more able to adapt. But, when conflict exists, when one home criticises the other, they may be interrogated, expected to pass on information, and this does cause problems.

> "I used to hate going home. I knew when I got there they would ask me all about what they've got, what washing machine, what's in the house, how may bedrooms, how much did the house cost, etc. As I got home, I used to quickly go upstairs to my room to escape it."

Children develop ways to cope with these conflicts. They become defensive, uncommunicative, afraid in fact to say anything lest they get one or the other parent into trouble. They develop *'watertight compartments in their minds'*. There is a grave risk that their values will be distorted and damaged by parents who cannot appreciate that such behaviour is influencing their future.

> "I had to lie to my mum. She used to talk my dad down all the time. I find it hard to trust women."

"Don't quiz or interrogate your child about their other parent. Learn to mind your own business!"

Even if parents can manage to reduce their own conflict in order to shield their children, there still may be insecurity and fear of what the future holds. When parents are unable to manage the situation reasonably, for whatever reason, children are at greater risk.

Children still need both parents

The key factor is accepting their need of a continuing relationship with all those they knew and loved before the break-up of their parent's relationship. All should encourage them to benefit from this network of support. Security and stability is not simply having one home to live in; it is a state of mind.

"They need to know you both still love them unconditionally, despite your own problems."

Managing family changes in a child-centred manner is not easy. It may take many years to come to terms with the breakdown of the relationship. Both parents can feel insecure, hurt and angry, and especially fear 'losing' their children. As each attempts to do what they consider to be best, they may not realise how confusing it can be for children. Being the centre of so much love and attention can become an overwhelming responsibility.

"Make them secure. Tell them you'll always be there for them."

Awareness of possible problems for children is one thing: being able to do anything to prevent the damage is quite another. If your children live mainly elsewhere, how do you manage?

MAKING THE BEST OF BEING THE 'OTHER' PARENT

As with most things, a positive attitude can make a difference. If you are negative, if you fear rejection or failure, or if you don't recognise and deal firmly with behaviour that may harm your relationship with your children, they will lose out.

If you can remain focused on what your child needs from you in the short- and long-term, if you are determined to make the best of whatever opportunities there are to contribute to their lives, if you refuse to give up, your children will benefit.

Your attitude rubs off on them: their behaviour is affected by yours. You and they may not realise this at the time, especially if conflicts arise or if you see little of one another, but eventually, they will make sense of it all, look back and realise how much you cared, how hard you tried.

Be positive about your 'ex' partner

(Through gritted teeth if need be!)

Your relationship with the other parent is going to be the biggest single thing that affects all your lives until your children become independent.

The breakdown of a once loving relationship does result in changed attitudes. However, one parent cannot simply be cast off, considered to be less important – imagine the gap in children's lives. FNF fathers who have not seen their child for months worry that the child will forget them, but regardless of lost time together, children do not forget their dads.

> *"A father went off to war, returning many months later. His young son ran towards him and jumped into his arms."*

The key influence is the attitude of the other parent. They will give out either positive or negative signals. Children soon sense when all is 'OK', and they will react accordingly. If they sense that one parent disapproves of the other, they face difficult choices.

*"All the photos of their dad were taken out of the album.
They were told not to say his name."*

Children need a positive image of both their parents. Many parents die when their children are young; children can and do manage without them. The difference is that the surviving parent will want to keep a positive memory alive. The extended family also rallies round rather than taking 'sides'. So often when families break down, this is the opposite of what happens. Even when arrangements and relationships begin from a reasonable footing, an event, a move, a change of whatever kind can suddenly put this in jeopardy. Some people unfortunately have to face animosity from the start. Sometimes it is a one-sided battle, one parent having no choice but to face the flack. Whichever situation you find yourself in, no matter what you have to deal with, positive thought and action creates more opportunities. How you conduct yourself also makes a difference. There are occasions when your behaviour may be misjudged (Walking on eggshells, p31).

The parents who have fed their experiences into this book understand how difficult it can be to negotiate with the other parent. The next section is based on their positive suggestions, plus thoughts on what to avoid.

CONSIDERATION, CO-OPERATION, COMPROMISE, COMMUNICATION

Be considerate and listen

If you don't listen to each other, you have virtually no chance of reaching agreement. How will you work out what the problem is? It must be said that either parent can become confrontational. Ultimately, without a real desire to listen to each other, to take on board the issues that each finds important, you will not move forward. If the other parent chooses not to listen, it's still best to choose the less adversarial route, unless of course, the child is at risk, for example if they are not free to continue their relationship with the rest of their family. If this happens, you must find ways to help them.

Co-operate

Try to be flexible even if it means making compromises. Everything can become competitive, no one prepared to back down lest this shows weakness, especially if that weakness might then be exploited by the 'other side'. Focus on the effect all this uncertainty will have upon children. The example set, the way those they are closest to resolve the problems, will undoubtedly have an influence upon their future behaviour. For their sakes, try to show you are prepared to try to work with the other parent.

Compromise

It's impossible miraculously to make a contentious situation perfect for all. Compromises are needed all round. They are easier to accept if everyone understands what's happening, and if it is accepted that all are making a positive effort to reach agreement. Focus on long-term aims and be prepared to give way sometimes in order to achieve these. Don't expect things to be sorted out quickly. It can be a slow process, gradually improving arrangements, clearing up misconceptions and building trust (between all concerned, including others that may become involved).

Open up channels of communication

If you cannot talk to one another, there is a real danger that attitudes will harden and decisions will be based on assumptions, not facts. Try not to jump to conclusions or immediately think the worst. It is so easy to project your own anxiety, disapproval and insecurity upon your children, especially when you are still suffering from the separation and perhaps feel let down. Unresolved emotional turmoil causes all kinds of over-reactions, including preventing children spending time with their other parent. Parents having problems re-adjusting need help to focus on how this is harmful for the children. Try to empathise with the other parent – they will also be feeling insecure. It takes time to adjust: *both of you will have to adapt to being apart from children.* Watching you 'take them away' may not be easy.

> "Look out for opportunities to have calm discussions with the ex. They are not angry all the time!"

Even if you think it will be pointless, don't be afraid to make contact with your ex-partner or his or her family. There is no way you can predict the reaction, so don't make assumptions: you may get it very wrong. Perhaps arrange a meeting with a family friend or a neutral third party present. This may get some of the main misapprehensions out of the way and get dialogue re-started. If you can each acknowledge that *both* parents love their children, this is a good first aim.

Then, moving on from there, that children love and need *both* parents. There is less justification for denying loving relationships if these basics can be defined and agreed.

Give the benefit of the doubt

If there is little or no communication, you might not have enough information to judge what's really happening.

> *"She did this deliberately. She knows this is my weekend. Why couldn't she have at least phoned me?"*

When arrangements to collect children are disrupted, it is not easy to cope with the frustration and disappointment, especially if you have travelled hundreds of miles to be with them as some parents do. Try not to misjudge the motives of the other parent until you have had an opportunity to find out what went wrong.

If the disruption becomes a regular pattern or if the other parent refuses to discuss the situation, you must decide what you can do to improve things, especially for children. Don't back off, or just go away. If they are in the middle of this kind of situation, especially if they are young, they will be unable to judge what's happening. It will not help if you just disappear. They might end up thinking you abandoned them, didn't care. It may take many years for them to readjust their understanding of events.

Drawing the line

All the above advice about being flexible, trying to accommodate the needs of others is a good example for children too. However, sometimes you just have to say 'enough is enough'. You may be expected to agree to arrangements, etc. that you cannot realistically meet. Perhaps you will be asked to collect children at times that are really inconvenient, e.g. are incompatible with your working pattern. The other parent may push you to your limit. If you eventually decide to make it clear that you have done all you can, but are not prepared to give in yet again, they may realise they must change course. Be warned this can lead to threats of reprisals (usually about less or no time with children) unless demands are met. In FNF's experience, money issues are the source of a high proportion of disputes about arrangements for children.

A common time for such threats is after holiday arrangements have been agreed. Suddenly children will not be able to go with you unless certain conditions are met, e.g. *'Pay for this now, or they can't come.'* Children who had been looking forward to the holiday will be disappointed and uncertain. What should you do? If you decide that you must take some action to prevent further harm being done, consider carefully before issuing ultimatums. You are best placed to know the personality and possible reaction of the other parent. You must be prepared to take the consequences if things get worse. It is not easy to 'make waves', even when the reason for standing ground is really important. Weigh up how the children will be affected, depending on which course you choose. Remember they may get confusing signals about what is acceptable behaviour, be equally damaged if they watch one parent manipulate the other.

"They've been divorced for years but the whole of my life my dad has had to do what she wants him to do. It's a power struggle. He's such a pushover."

Reasonable behaviour may be perceived as weak: behaving unreasonably may be seen as getting results. Understandably, it can be difficult to find a 'right time' to discuss sensitive issues, especially if the time spent with children is limited. On the other hand, appeasing the other parent (or children) no matter how they behave, may simply be storing up problems for the future.

Admitting you make mistakes, but you still love your children

If you are responsible for the end of the relationship, for example if it was you who found another partner, it is inevitable that the parent 'left behind' will feel angry and resentful. The children may also feel betrayed or abandoned, and if the adults around them are less than tactful (be fair, it will be difficult for them not to be partisan), these feelings will be reinforced.

In these circumstances they may stop you seeing the children for a time. They may tell you that the children do not want to see you. This doesn't mean they do not love you. They may not fully understand what's happening. They need reassurance, to know that despite the relationship between their parents ending, you still love them and need them. Keep up some form of indirect contact with them during this difficult time. Don't assume they won't open your letters. Just seeing a letter arrive on the doormat is a start, even if they aren't allowed, or ready to read it.

One father advised getting all this out in the open, admitting you acted badly, asking your family to try to understand what happened and to forgive you. It takes a great deal of courage to do that, but you may all be able to move forward afterwards.

Keeping calm

When communication breaks down or becomes disjointed everyone will lose out.

Sometimes, despite your best efforts, the difficulties between you and the other parent may seem insurmountable. It is even more important to remain positive and calm, otherwise you could jeopardise whatever tenuous thread of contact you may have.

One father gave the following practical advice for dealing with difficult situations:

➤ *Keep calm/never ever answer back.*

➤ *Always be on time for pickup and drop off.*

➤ *Avoid becoming angry no matter how provoked.*

➤ *Where possible, arrange the hand-over of children on neutral public ground.*

➤ *No matter how tempted, do not express resentment of mother in front of children.*

➤ *Always remember to focus on being a loving father and not a resentful ex.*

➤ *Discreetly make notes of ugly scenes and unreasonable behaviour, with witnesses if you can, and keep a diary of events. This may be needed if things don't improve and you think your children are suffering.*

➤ *Use BT's '141' facility* when ringing the other parent (less excuse not to answer your call).*

➤ *Contact another FNF member for support if feeling suicidal or like giving up.*

➤ *Never give up in the view that it is better for the child – it is not!*

---

*BT users can use 141 to withhold their number on a call-by-call basis. Simply dial '141' in front of the number you're calling.

It is sad, but realistic to have to think of future repercussions should things go wrong, and you need proof of reasonable or unreasonable behaviour (of either parent). You must also be aware that your behaviour can easily be misinterpreted, and if judged as aggressive or angry, this may raise questions about your ability to look after your children. Take the advice in the next section very seriously.

WALKING ON EGGSHELLS

The time when children are collected or are taken back to the other parent can be stressful. It may be one of the few times parents meet face to face. Inevitably, each will be tense, anxious perhaps to raise issues that need discussing. More worrying are the times when tempers flare, and one parent or the other will be determined to score a point.

It is crucial to keep calm at these moments. Although it can be difficult when you have to deal with your own emotions, focus on the children. If either parent ends up shouting or swearing, the children will be upset, possibly frightened. Abuse such as *'They know you don't care about them'* can become a regular feature of the 'doorstep conversations'.

Children with their weekend carrier bags in hand are unable to escape although often they learn to ignore the conflict. Attempting to undermine the relationship with their other parent unnecessarily damages their self-confidence and causes anxiety.

Ironically, if the 'resident' parent gets angry with you, this is seldom perceived as causing problems for children. However, any behaviour on your part that can be interpreted as aggressive, including appearing angry, places you at risk of not being allowed to spend time with your children (Cafcass, p101).

Any behaviour likely to be interpreted by a court as intimidating may be sufficient to convince the court to make an order against you. Often no evidence of actual abuse is necessary: it is sufficient for the other parent to state they are/were afraid. This is especially relevant for those who are still living in the same home. Courts have wide-ranging powers to deal with family abuse. You may find yourself ousted from your home, and can be ordered not to go near your family.

Many FNF members report that professionals who may become involved (police, social services, health professionals, Cafcass, etc.) commonly seem to work from the presumption that it is the woman who needs protecting. This happens even when the children's mother has initiated a domestic incident and been abusive and/or physically violent. One father although abused and attacked on numerous occasions by his ex-partner, was sent literature asking him if he would like counselling for 'his' problem.

Where a mother refuses to allow children to be with their father, negative assumptions may also be made about the father's past behaviour.

"He must have done something to give her cause for concern about the children."

Although this ought to be unacceptable without evidence, in reality you will be the one who will have to prove your innocence. You *must* proceed with caution when dealing with a parent who is resisting your involvement, or any professionals who contact you. For example it is simply common sense not to go into the other parent's home on your own. Also make sure you have someone with you who can act as a witness if needs be.

If contact with the other parent results in confrontation, it is probably a good idea to work out other ways for the children to move between parents, to reduce the conflict for all.

"Try collecting children at a neutral venue. This is more natural than one parent 'taking' the children 'from' the other. It is normal to take or collect from school (make sure the school is aware). This avoids contact, possible conflict between parents. Even if parents are trying to work everything out for the children's sake, they may not be very friendly to each other."

Other members suggest arranging the 'transfer' via a child-minder or at a mutual friend's home. Meeting in a public place such as a supermarket or McDonalds can also reduce the likelihood of arguments – very sensible advice, if all are able to recognise the damage that can be done when children witness angry scenes. The biggest problem, as with all disputes between parents, is that one parent may have more power to control what happens. They may not want to change existing arrangements. If they refuse to co-operate, you have limited options.

Possible solutions

You could ask someone they trust to help you resolve the problem, perhaps a member of their family, a friend, a representative of their religious group. Some members of FNF have mediation or counselling experience and may be able to offer advice. You could try a mediation service (Mediation, p10). Local FNF members may be able to suggest which ones have been helpful.

If you have to seek legal advice go with a firm idea of what you want to achieve, i.e. less conflict for all, especially children, and not an aggressive and protracted legal battle. This will only make the lawyers rich, and make others more determined to 'win' (also see Part Three). Prepare a schedule that would result in fewer problems for children. FNF may be able to help with this.

Ultimately, you must convince the court that you are concerned about the effects upon the child and as such are trying to improve current arrangements. It is acknowledged that those hearing such applications, having to make decisions where families cannot agree, do not have any magic solutions. They are therefore faced with difficult decisions. Time allowed for hearings or the preparation of welfare reports (Cafcass p101) is rarely sufficient to explore background history or problems, or the options available, therefore any positive input on your part must be beneficial. Also, be aware that there are extensive powers to check information held by other agencies, e.g. the police. Be prepared for anything alleged to count against you.

Freedom and risk

It can be extremely difficult to differentiate between personal feelings about what environment, company you would *prefer* your child to be in, and what is actually harmful. When there is little or no real communication, there is much scope for misinterpretation of motives and reality. The 'truth' is often difficult to establish.

It is easy to over-react; for example, some might find the slightest excuse to reduce the time children can spend with their other parent. Others might decide they should apply for the children to live with them. It is easy for mums or dads to become paranoid about the other parent's inadequacies.

"I 'disapproved' of the way she'd over-react to every sniffle, yet when I knew my child was at risk, no one would take me seriously."

'Good enough' is good enough: don't expect perfection. Every parent makes mistakes, but it is more constructive to focus on what they positively contribute to the lives of their children. Being constantly critical is destructive and influences children adversely. It may undermine their relationship with their other parent and anyone else they share time with in that parent's home, e.g. new partners, stepparents, other children (New partners, p77).

Although it is sometimes hard not to feel possessive about children, *they must feel free to have an ongoing relationship with both their parents and the rest of their family*. It is this freedom that is infinitely more important than how much time they spend with each parent, or even the 'quality' of that time spent together.

MAKING THE MOST OF TIME TOGETHER OR APART

Whatever your situation, maintaining a relationship with children after you and the other parent no longer live together is far from straightforward. It is natural to want to make the most of the precious time with children not seen very often. This does not mean that they have to have a 'mega' experience whenever they spend time with you. It can be difficult to strike a balance.

"Don't rush them. Learn to just relax with them. Do nothing, sit around, watch TV. So-called 'quality time' isn't just about having fun."

The most important aspect is the relationship between you and your children. It may be the most basic things you will do together that build a lasting memory. One dad was living in a rented flat without a washing machine (fathers often end up in poorly equipped accommodation). When his young son came to stay, they would go to the launderette, put the washing in the machine, then sit eating fish and chips on a wall outside. Not exciting stuff, but years later his son often asks, *'Do you remember when we used to go to the launderette?'* He sees this as the good times spent just with his dad.

Accommodation

When you first divorce or separate from the other parent, a decision has to be made about the division of the (often limited) family assets. Many fathers assume they have no alternative but to move out of the family home, are even advised to do so by solicitors. FNF would generally advise them not to move out, especially if arrangements for children to spend time with both parents have not been worked out. It may even be presented as desertion and count against you later. Accommodation for children is the first priority, as it should be, but their housing needs do not necessarily require only 'one base'. The pattern of life will be different for everyone after parents eventually move apart. If children are to continue to have both parents fully involved in their lives, they will need to spend time with both parents, in their respective homes. They can and do adapt to moving between their two home bases.

Being able to have your children to stay with you is essential if you are to keep your relationship intact. It is seldom acknowledged that many fathers cannot afford suitable accommodation for their children after families split up. Taking children to McDonalds or out for a pizza is easily perceived as spoiling children, and can cause friction especially if the other parent is unable to afford to do this. But catering for children can be a real problem when living in a bedsit. Not having room for children to stay overnight also seriously limits the amount and quality of time together. They will need their own space, however basic, with both parents. Put forward the argument that children are less likely to be free to retain their relationship with you – and may even be denied this – if there is not suitable accommodation for them to stay with you (Cafcass, p101). If a court orders that there should be one 'main' home, the costs incurred by the parent travelling to and from that home *should* be taken into account. If maintenance is calculated under CMEC (Child Maintenance and Enforcement Commission, p72) there are different rules depending on when your family was first assessed. For example, pre-March 03 (the 'old scheme'), no allowance was made for these essential costs. Subsequent reforms for new cases from March 03 enabled the parent paying child support to apply for a reduction if they have 'exceptional contact costs'. (Legislation in this area is complex and evolving. Refer to FNF's website for current information.)

Being realistic, mothers will probably assume that children should live with them. The need for you to provide (and fund) additional accommodation elsewhere may not be taken on board. They may also feel insecure about their own housing needs and how they will manage financially.

It is hard to come to terms with the fact that standards of living will drop, as they inevitably will when parents split up. Both parents need time to adjust to their new situations. At such times, it is difficult to focus on the needs of the children. However, *if overall responsibility can be shared between you, there are obvious benefits for all, especially your children.*

Shared Residence Orders are becoming more common (p90). This is impacting on other areas of life post-separation, e.g. rights to state benefits and local authority housing, customarily given to one parent only. As test cases are heard in the courts, new precedents are being set. For example, several years ago, a father with a Shared Residence Order appealed against a judgement that he would not be given family accommodation for his children, even though they would be spending an equal amount of time with him. Briefly, the local authority had argued that the children would be 'living' with one parent, but only 'staying' with the other parent. In Oct 2007, the Court of Appeal dismissed this argument. The local authority then took the case to the House of Lords, where the judgement was overturned. However, local authorities still have a requirement to pay housing benefit on a discretionary basis and in accordance with equality and other primary legislation.

You can see from the above, that progress is seldom straightforward, plus even if test cases are successful, the impact they have on practices takes time to filter through to everyday life. As said throughout this guide, *you cannot always guarantee that those dealing with your family situation are up-to-date with the latest legal or policy guidance. If you meet a brickwall when applying for benefits or accommodation for your children, it's worth double-checking the current position.*

Children's possessions, etc.

What happens about their toys, clothes, etc.? You may be reluctant to let them take these to their other home. Older children especially may resent any interference – a gift is not a gift if there are conditions attached. It's probably better not to be too rigid about most things. If you decide that you would prefer some major items to remain at your home, explain that it's not practical to keep buying replacements, and they will need some familiar things at your home and something to play with next time they are with you. You can always re-assess the situation if it doesn't work out.

Clothing is a more complex issue. Who buys what for where causes lots of ill-feeling. It is not unheard of for children to arrive for a fortnight's stay with only one set of clothes. Keeping spare clothes specifically for wearing at your home is common sense. Be sure to return any clothing that your child brings. You will not be popular if you send everything back unwashed. However, one father reported that the other parent objected to the smell of the fabric conditioner that his new partner used. There will be times when you just can't win! Always remember to return other essentials such as homework and school items. Children frequently forget what they brought in the first place. If your relationship with the other parents is tense, you may get the blame. Children can also be very upset if they think they will be told off. One six-year-old became really anxious about returning exactly the same supermarket carrier bag his mum had used for his clothes. There have been many cases where children were prevented from being with their other parent following an argument over something comparatively trivial.

Distance between homes

The distance between you and the other parent is obviously going to play a major part in how you arrange to share responsibility, and organise time with children. Many parents will complain bitterly that their children have been moved from North London to South London, necessitating a trip across the Thames. Others accept with equanimity a move from London to Norwich or Birmingham as awkward, but not too unreasonable.

It really is a question of what you can manage, what you are prepared to do to keep the relationship with your children active. Many, many FNF members travel vast distances, regularly. They do this simply because they are parents, couldn't imagine being anything else. The expenses and time involved shape their lives, often leaving them very short of money. New partners may be unable to deal with the commitment and stress. Travelling regularly between children's homes is expensive: poorer fathers often just cannot afford the cost. There is, however, little recognition or sympathy for relatively poor dads, and state benefits, although very accessible to mothers (presumed to be the 'main carer'), are not equally available to fathers.

When children are moved away

Travelling between homes within the UK, or indeed anywhere, becomes more of a problem when the long weekend visit becomes untenable. When it is first discovered that the 'ex' intends to take the children off to live somewhere else, the immediate reaction is, *'Surely they can't do that?'* Unfortunately, despite the principles in legislation concerning children (Legal framework, p89) they almost always assume they can, and move regardless, and this fact is one of the most poignant examples of the inequality between mums and dads.

If persuasion against such a move has failed, the objecting parent can (some would say, should) apply for a court order preventing the move. The other parent may apply to the court to remove the children *'from the jurisdiction'* (outside England and Wales). The court will probably still give permission for permanent removal of a child from the jurisdiction if proposals can be shown to be 'reasonable' and 'realistic', and are 'consistent with the child's welfare'. The court has wide discretion, and should take the 'wishes and feelings' of children into account. However, UK case law (past court judgements) shows that mothers are almost always given leave to take children to live abroad, even though being able to remain in contact with their father is made difficult or even impossible. One very young child was taken to live in the USA. Her father who lived in the UK was granted *'not more than one extended weekend per month'* (e.g. Friday, Saturday and Sunday), and *'not less than two hours on each weekend day'* – all to take place in the USA. Any further contact was *'subject to reasonable negotiations between the parties'*.

He was unable to re-negotiate this arrangement and therefore spent many hours travelling back and forth across the Atlantic every month to be with his daughter for just a snatch of time.

The legal situation here is some way off that in other countries where greater emphasis is placed upon sharing responsibility and care, and where *both* parents have to respect the children's right to a continuing relationship with their family.

To quote a senior Florida judge:

> **"Neither parent shall be in the driver's seat."**

Holidays overseas

If you do not have PR, you will have to get the other parent's permission for anything concerning your children, including holidays abroad.

If you have Parental Responsibility and there are no other orders in force then you have equal legal status with the mother and can in theory take your children anywhere you like on holiday. However, it is an offence for any person to take children out of the UK without 'appropriate consent' (Abduction Act, next section).

If you have a Residence Order or a Shared Residence Order (p90), you can take your child out of the UK for up to one month without seeking consent. However, anyone else who has PR can apply for a Prohibited Steps Order (p90) to stop you, if they choose to do so (also see Abduction below). To repeat, it makes sense and can avert possible misunderstandings if you get prior agreement.

If there is a Residence Order in favour of another person then you cannot take children from the UK unless you have the written consent of that person and every other person who has PR, or have obtained leave of the court, e.g. by Specific Issue Order (p90).

To holiday abroad you will also need a valid passport for the child. New rules on children's passports came into force in 1998 – children can no longer be added to a parent's passport but are issued with their own. Any person with PR can apply (but must notify all others with PR).

Abduction

The Child Abduction Act 1984 makes it an offence to take or send a child out of the UK to live abroad without the appropriate consent from everyone who has PR for the child or leave of the court. The maximum penalty for a conviction is seven years' imprisonment.

If your child is taken to live abroad without your consent or in breach of a court order, you may apply for a return under the Hague Convention on International Child Abduction, if a contracting state is involved. A return will enable you to have the case heard in the UK courts.

If you fear an international move, it is vital that you immediately apply to a British court to establish jurisdiction. If you do not and the move is presented as a permanent one, the children may be deemed to be habitually resident in their new country almost immediately. You may find it very difficult to mount a case for residence and contact in a court overseas. These are highly technical matters, and *if you think this might happen to your family, immediately contact the relevant voluntary or government body best equipped to give you specific advice* (Part Four, Nos 5, 25 & 45).

Practical considerations

However the move overseas comes about, whichever route you choose to resolve the problems, children will want to see you just as much when they find themselves in Bolivia as when they were still up the road. The logistics of maintaining the relationship become entirely dependent on money, time available and co-operation. If co-operation is happening, then costs and travel can be shared, together with telephone calls and incidentals like passports, visas, etc. Young children need to be accompanied when travelling and this burden is halved if both parents pitch in. You will need information about what you can and can't do legally and what welfare benefits are available (start with the Citizens Advice Bureau).

> "People need basic information about 'unaccompanied minors' on aeroplanes, risks of unaccompanied travel in general, child fares on transport, cheap telephone accounts for international calls, family railcards, best bed & breakfast guide, possibly get a camper van if children are still in the UK, getting child benefit if the ex is abroad, check out which airline has the best approach to kids. Some have individual TVs for each seat, essential when kids want to watch something nobody else wants or can't see the big screen over the top of the seat in front, etc., etc."

As this shows, the increasing numbers of FNF members who have children living abroad are undoubtedly the best people to ask about all the practical details. They report that some airlines for instance, are increasingly geared up to children travelling alone and children actually enjoy the independence.

As said before the prospects of stopping a move abroad are slim. Some would therefore advise negotiating as good a deal on parenting time, costs and child support as possible. This can save everyone costly and counter-productive legal action.

With hostile ex-partners, where no negotiation is possible and the object of moving may be to disown the other parent, then the situation is dire as the following account shows:

"I tried to get her to go to mediation in the USA (which costs $200 an hour plus the cost of drawing up a mediation agreement at the end – I offered to pay) to sort out the arrangements for our child. My ex said that she was not interested in mediation. I had actually booked a whole week in the States in August, to allow time for mediation, only to be told afterwards that she wasn't interested. As I couldn't change my ticket, I had to spend the time there but wasn't allowed to see my daughter one minute over the minimum time allocated by the court."

If circumstances allow, it may be easier for you to move too. This may seem drastic, but on the plus side, the legal system in many other countries, e.g. Australia and *some* parts of the USA are more father-friendly and the chances of a court order enabling your children to spend time with you are greater. Legislation varies from State to State: attitudes and practices will be different in each one. Always make sure you check the most up-to-date local information about the system in whatever countries or regions apply in your situation.

'Indirect contact'

This term is common shorthand to describe staying in contact with your child when you are not able to be together for any length of time (be that a day, a week, or longer).

When all else fails, or the geographical distance between you and your children is unavoidable, communicating in other ways, such as by letter and phone calls, can keep your relationship alive.

From one of FNF's Parent support workshops:

This is the moon up here. I've put the moon there because when I'm talking to my daughter and she's in Wisconsin and I'm in West Sussex and we're talking on the telephone, we're 4,000 miles apart, and it feels like a very long way. But it's an amazing thing for both people to be able to stand at the window and look out and both see the moon at the same moment. It's a common reference. It's very difficult when you're separated that far from somebody, who's probably the only person in your life you're prepared to die for, immediately without question. It's that strange dichotomy...someone who is so important, someone that you can't separate from mentally and emotionally, and yet be so physically separate in distance and time.

Do all you can to try to reassure them that, although apart, you are still thinking about them, even if you are concerned that the other parent may block your attempts to communicate. *You may not be confident that children will receive your letters, but write anyway. Keep copies, so that in the future you can reassure them that you didn't just give up.*

Don't expect children to write you thank-you letters for presents and so on. They don't usually spontaneously write anything – or say 'thank you' – until they are quite old, unless an adult encourages them. If you do not get a thank-you, it is not the child's fault. It does not mean they are not pleased to have your messages and gifts. And if they write, or say that they do not want to hear from you anymore or to have your presents, etc., it may be because they have been told to do this. This reflects the difficult position they are in (Parental alienation, p82).

Even young children may suspect all is not quite right, and actually resent the invasion of their privacy.

"I remember thinking that she (Mum) had a cheek opening my letters. Think she was afraid of him (Dad) saying anything that might set us against her. He never did – just used to ask how she was. Dad was determined: he never missed my birthday. He told me to phone and reverse the charges."

You could try phoning regularly, but again it is easy to prevent calls getting through, simply by leaving the answer machine on (try dialling '141': p30).

"It was hard to do because I really wanted to know what was being said but, I used to encourage my children to ring

42

their mum, and I made sure I was out of earshot while they did. Parents should allow their children privacy to contact the other parent."

It is not easy to be relaxed when speaking to a child you may not see often, and they may not be able to speak freely either, if someone is listening. If they seem distant, it isn't because they don't want to hear from you. Their priorities are different. You may have called in the middle of the favourite TV programme, or when their friends are with them. If they live in a different country, phoning across time-zones is particularly difficult, especially if you don't know what activities, etc. they are involved in. You could decide on a signal; for example, your child could telephone, letting the phone ring for three rings, then hang up. That would let you know that it's 'OK' to ring.

It can be relatively inexpensive to call long distance: find out what deals are currently available. There are Internet sites that offer cheaper calls when prefixing numbers dialled with their codes. You could buy them a phone card or even a mobile phone if you can afford it. This does make things a bit less complicated for them. Don't be disappointed if they don't often ring or text: at least they have the opportunity. Computers are greatly improving the prospects for all to keep in touch. Children who would never contact you by phone or writing a letter may be more familiar with sending emails. They may also be able to use software packages (MSN, Skype, iChat, etc.) to make calls over the Internet. Your children may possibly be unsupervised for some of the time, so this could be a relatively private way for you both to communicate. But be aware that they may well be anxious to avoid the other parent finding out. Internet chat sites also open up opportunities for sharing news. Many people have set up their own personal or family website. FNF receives reports that children thought 'lost' do eventually make contact with their families.

There are many fathers who have had restrictions placed on their 'indirect contact' with their children. They may be expected to phone only so many times in a given period, or at very specific times. Some have been ordered not to contact their children at all, even though they are decent, caring parents. This can happen when it is claimed that the other parent finds any contact upsetting. It is 'justified' on the grounds that 'upsetting the mother might upset the child'. The fact that the child's relationship with its other parent might be damaged seems to be of lesser importance (NB: The UK *should* uphold the UN Convention on the Rights of the Child, including the right to be cared for by both parents – UNICEF: Part Four, No 29). However, if you are ordered indirect contact only, ask for a review after a short period to be built in. *If you cannot change things, continue to do whatever you can short-term, and focus on the hope of improvements. As your children get older, it will be easier for them to make their own decisions.*

It is perhaps also a good idea to take stock of what may be a comfortable routine for you, but perhaps no longer suits everyone else. Many have recommended regularly reviewing arrangements to adapt to children's and adults' changing needs and circumstances. Children often have strong views on this, but they can be the last to be asked. They may not be free to volunteer an opinion.

> "Mary was told Dad wanted to reduce her time with him to once a month because he didn't want to do all the travelling involved. She found out years later that it was Mum who made the decision, not Dad (Mum's new partner didn't like Dad appearing so regularly). Mary missed seeing her Dad, but didn't say anything at the time, thinking Dad didn't care. Nobody thought to ask her. Even if they had, what would she have said?"

Research suggests that children desperately want to be informed. You should talk to them, and crucially, listen to what they say and ask. Give honest answers about what is happening and why, even if it appears to contradict what others are saying. That way, children can work things out for themselves. It might give them the courage to speak out if their views and feelings are not being considered. But they will not want to hear you openly criticising their other parent...that's a no-go area, hands-over-the-ears territory. *Don't go there at the expense of your children, no matter how you feel.*

PART TWO: Being realistic

GETTING TO GRIPS

This section will touch on some situations you may have to deal with. *"I thought I was the only one..."* is a comment frequently made by newcomers to FNF. Working through some of the problems that can arise as you and the other parent try to re-shape your lives apart can be time-consuming, stressful and demoralising. Take comfort from the fact that others have had similar experiences and understand how you might react, and more importantly, have a more realistic idea of what you can and can't change. Hopefully, their insights may prepare you for some of the unknowns, and help you decide what's best for you and your family. FNF also has a series of guides and leaflets on a wide range of issues (see Part Four). The FNF local contact volunteers can also help, and the charity also has an Internet Discussion Forum where members can share experiences, ask for advice and find out how others deal with a variety of 'separation' issues. FNF's National Telephone Helpline is also available.

You will need to consider how attitudes to men and childcare might affect your decisions. *It is a myth that men cannot look after children.* You will need to be prepared to challenge common assumptions, and perhaps your own views on what dads can do.

CARING FOR CHILDREN

When parents no longer live together, there is a major adjustment necessary, by all concerned. Each will have to adapt to having sole responsibility while the child is with them.

Be confident

Caring for children is often regarded as 'women's work'. *Men are often the first to believe this.* A dad recently said that he thought his wife was *'instinctively better'* at doing all the caring especially when his child was young. It could be argued (and was by his wife) that this has nothing to do with instinct, but simply the amount of time spent with either parent. This is also reinforced when Dad takes a crying child back to Mum to 'make it better'. Being seen as the parent with the magic wand is very satisfying. Women still assume the main caring responsibility for children within a relationship, often because they prefer to do so. That does not mean that men are not equally capable of performing the same tasks for children.

> "Michael has sole care of his three-year-old son. He works full time, lives a fair distance from his work. He has no relatives nearby who might otherwise have helped. He therefore decided to find childcare facilities near where he works. His son spends the day at a nursery. Michael sees him at lunchtime, takes him to the park, etc. When they get home, Michael deals with all the other chores that need to be done."

Looking after children is not a magic science; it just needs practice and determination to care as best you can for your children. *If you get it wrong sometimes, so what?* If there were a blueprint for raising children perfectly, the inventor would have made a fortune.

If you are unused to taking charge of all the aspects of childcare, don't panic! Get some advice, ask your friends, family: buy some magazines. The SureStart booklet *Looking for Childcare?* (Part Four, No 73) is a good starting point for anyone needing an overview of government policy, rights to free places, options, costs, who to contact for information, etc. It also lists contact information for the local authority that can help with what's available in your area. They keep lists of registered child-minders, nurseries, toy libraries, etc.

Sharing the care of children means that some dads (and mums) have to re-assess and re-organise their working patterns. This is a good thing, allowing both parents an opportunity to broaden their input into their children's lives. Some may choose less demanding jobs, or work flexi-hours, so that they can be available when they are needed. Employers have to take on board the concept of men needing childcare facilities, or time off when children are ill or to go to school events, etc. It is becoming more common for men to arrange their working lives around children, and change is essential as an increasing number of families have similar needs. It is illegal to discriminate by gender of parent.

Employers must provide the same facilities for your children whether you are a mother or father (Part Four, Nos 37 & 41).

Flexible working

If you have Parental Responsibility for children under the age of six (or disabled children under the age of eighteen) you (and your partner) have the right to apply to your employer to work more flexibly. This can cover hours of work, times and place of work, and requests for different patterns of work. The request must be made in writing and your employer can refuse it only if there are clear business grounds for doing so. Up-to-date information from Directgov (Government Departments, p123).

Unpaid parental leave

Parental leave gives 'qualifying' parents the right to take *unpaid* time off work to look after children under five (eighteen if they are disabled). In December 1999 new fathers were for the first time given a right to thirteen weeks unpaid parental leave, to be taken during the first five years of the child's life (for employees with at least one year's continuous service).

The leave is available to all mothers, all married fathers, unmarried fathers who have obtained Parental Responsibility, and adoptive parents. If twins are born each parent may take thirteen weeks leave for each child. Employees remain employed while on parental leave and are guaranteed the right to return to the same (if leave taken is less than four weeks) or similar job. If you are divorced or separated and don't live with the other parent this does not affect the right to take parental leave (for full and current information: Part Four, Nos 4, 30, 37 & 41).

Paid paternity leave

(The conditions for claiming this are complex: more references below.)

The basics: you can claim either one week or two consecutive weeks' paid paternity leave (not odd days) if you are:

> *An employed father who has or expects to have responsibility for the child's upbringing*
> *The biological father of the child, or the mother's husband or partner*
> *The child's adopter or the partner of the adopter*

And if you have:

> ➢ *Worked continuously for your employer for twenty-six weeks ending with the 15th week before the baby is due, or if you have adopted a child, the end of the week in which you were matched with the child.*

Leave must be taken within fifty-six days of the actual date of birth of the child, or if the child is born early, within the period from the actual date of birth up to fifty-six days after the first day of the week in which the birth was expected.

There are earnings thresholds and other conditions. The Directgov website has further information, including an interactive tool to help you assess whether you qualify (Part Four, p123). ACAS can also advise (Part Four, No 4).

State benefits

Caring for children is expensive. Both parents with care of children should check out the range of benefits. Find out what's available (the Citizens Advice Bureau should be able to help). While there are many state benefits available to parents, divorced or separated fathers often complain of difficulty in claiming them. The system is still largely geared to one 'primary carer' (usually presumed to be the mother, or whoever can prove he or she has the greater share of care). It is an 'all or nothing' approach that is too inflexible to cope with the increasing number of children who have parents living in two separate homes. It is also geared to whole weeks of care, and only nights count. Therefore, if your shared care arrangements do not fit this pattern, for instance if your children are with you all day, but not overnight, you may lose out. One significant precedent is a 2004 court ruling that stated where a Shared Residence Order is in place, state benefits should be available to both parents caring for children.

> *"There is in my view no longer on the face of it any reason, if there ever was, why fathers who are parties to such arrangements should be placed at a financial disadvantage by the social security legislation."*
> (Lord Justice Scott Baker)

Despite this progress towards parental equality, please note that at the date of this publication, nothing has been done to improve the rules and regulations governing benefits. Child benefit is still provided to one parent by default, giving access to all other state benefits including local authority housing benefit. Where care is shared, one parent is still likely to be at a disadvantage.

Don't be put off: if you think you should be entitled to help with the responsibilities of raising your family, make a claim. It can be a time-consuming process convincing officials of your entitlement. Eventually, the system will have to adapt, but change is a slow process, with unavoidable cost implications.

Some tax allowances (e.g. Children's Tax Credits) are awarded to the parent who has 'main responsibility', with the expectation that separated parents will (and are able to) decide this between themselves fairly.

> If you share the responsibility for a child with another person who is not your partner, only one of you will be able to claim the Child Tax Credit for that child. You must decide which of you has the main responsibility for the child and that person should claim. You can consider the amount of time the child lives with you when deciding who has the main responsibility.
>
> HM Revenue & Customs (HMRC)

Where care is shared equally, the whole tax allowance is given to the household with the lowest income. If you fail to reach agreement with the other parent, contact the HMRC Tax Credits Helpdesk (Part Four, No 44).

Gender Equality Duty and public authorities

The Single Equality Act 2006 introduced the Gender Equality Duty (GED). This requires public bodies to promote and take action to bring about equal treatment for men and women.

A 'public authority' means any organisation, authority or institution operating within the public sector. This covers, for example, government departments, schools and other educational institutions, health services, benefit provision and local authority housing departments. The Equalities and Human Rights Commission has comprehensive information, including on their website: 'Enforcing the gender equality duty – A toolkit for individuals' (Part Four, No 62). This can help you assess whether local authorities are complying with the GED, plus actions to take if they fail to do so.

Legislation and policy are never static, so seek as much up-to-date information as you can, preferably before you have resigned yourself to your child being brought up mainly by the other parent. Sharing the care shares the responsibility, gives both parents more opportunities to work at the next step in their lives, move on.

Resistance

> "I know hundreds of fathers and have yet to meet one who can't gently hold his child or change its nappies, whatever is needed. In cases where a father might need genuine help with managing his baby this can be provided much better in a setting where the emphasis is on enabling rather than controlling."

Unfortunately, not all you meet may see it quite like this. If you cannot agree about arrangements for sharing care, you will find that mothers are universally regarded as being 'entitled to contact'. 'Separated' fathers are routinely expected to 'prove' they are still fit to look after their children. There appears to be a general reluctance to trust dads with children. The younger the children, the more resistance you may encounter.

It is irrational to be so over-cautious. Every day, fathers look after babies. It is also common for very young children to stay with other members of the family. As said earlier *children are adaptable. They can quickly adjust to new routines, will move between their parents quite happily if encouraged to do so*.

You will not be able to persuade all that you are (still) a capable parent. Don't expect support even if you have previously been the sole carer. Presumptions about what is 'natural' are commonplace. The other parent may be the most difficult to convince. It is common for courts, Cafcass (p101), etc. to be influenced by the mother's fears. Sometimes the motives for resisting your involvement have less to do with apprehension over childcare issues, but more to do with insecurity, i.e. fear of losing the children, or the result of more negative motives such as revenge.

If there are doubts put forward about your ability to look after your children, the court may suggest that a relative or friend, or even a Cafcass officer (p102) should be with you when you are with your child. The place and time you meet may be clearly defined. It can be extremely traumatic to have to interact with your children under such artificial circumstances. It is also not ideal for them either.

> "One dad said that the (maternal) grandmother would not at first let him feed his baby. Eventually she did let him do so, but would check to see if he had washed his hands first. He persevered, and gradually

was 'allowed' to take his child out for an hour or so (with granny in attendance). It was the mother who insisted that gran should be there."

Allegations of abuse

Domestic abuse, and abuse of children are very sensitive issues. Children need to be protected when there is evidence that they are at risk. If you are a father, it can be difficult to convince the 'powers that be' that a mother is harming a child. You also risk upsetting what may already be precarious parenting time arrangements. The risk to the child is the first priority. First of all, be as certain as you can that the risk is real (Freedom and risk, p33).

Sometimes allegations of misconduct, or abuse of either ex-partner or children are made where there is no evidence of risk, e.g. no history of abusive behaviour.

"My solicitor described allegations as routine."

This routine practice has also been described as 'the ultimate weapon', recognised within the legal system as a means to prolong the court proceedings, often after all other attempts to thwart a parent's involvement have failed. If the court is concerned about risk to children, even where the 'evidence' is simply based on the word of a 'concerned' person, they must investigate claims made. Given that it is the duty of the court to protect children, there is a tendency to err on the side of caution.

Many such claims evaporate once investigated but they can still influence what happens afterwards. One father was suddenly accused of sexually abusing his child in the latter part of the divorce proceedings: the claims were not substantiated. The mother still insisted that a relation should temporarily supervise whilst he was with his child. Over a year later, this was still happening. The father could go back to court but is concerned that this might cause more conflict, perhaps even less parenting time. He is therefore resigned to the current arrangements, hoping for improvements as the child gets older.

The many ordinary, decent, caring parents that have been falsely accused can testify to the damaging consequences especially for their relationship with their children. When the other parent is determined to stop a child spending time with their other parent, they may be tempted to use desperate measures. Be aware that an accusation might be made but don't become paranoid. *It is important to keep this in proportion, not let it interfere with what should be a relaxed and loving relationship with your children.*

If it does become an issue in your case, you must take it seriously. Just be aware that anything might be misconstrued, used against you.

> "A father phoned to ask for advice about his very young daughter. When he collected the child from its mother, he was given some cream that had to be applied for nappy rash. The relationship between the parents was tense. He was in tears because he was terrified that by applying the cream, he might be accused of sexual abuse."

The advice he was given for his protection was to ask a female neighbour to treat the nappy rash, just in case his motives were misinterpreted. Fathers now routinely change nappies, bath their children, etc. This is encouraged, regarded as 'normal'. It is only when the relationship between the parents breaks down that motives may be questioned. It is really sad that this affects what is an everyday caring relationship between parents and children.

Sometimes a child's innocent and obviously unoriginal remark can fuel unfounded fears and prompt an over-reaction.

> "A young child's parents were unable to agree about arrangements for their child to spend time with both of them. The mother was resisting his involvement, and Dad had applied for a contact order. One day the child was at nursery and said, 'Daddy's a b*****d'. The mother later used this statement (with the nursery staff's support) to claim that the child didn't want to see his dad. Eventually an expert was appointed to interview the child. The child was asked, 'What is the worst thing your daddy has done to you?"

The question should have been: 'Where did the child pick up a phrase like that?' Clearly any investigations thought necessary should be done sensitively bearing in mind that children (especially young ones) are apt to repeat things without understanding meanings or implications. If asked leading questions, they often try to give the answer they think is expected of them. Children should not have to take responsibility for whether they 'want' to see their other parent. The innocent father and child above no longer have any contact. Having exhausted every avenue attempting to re-start their relationship he is now disillusioned and despairing. It is no consolation that all may have been done with the best intentions.

Undoubtedly, there should be a way to deal with these cases more equitably. However, faced with the reality of an investigation into your family, you will in effect have to prove yourself innocent, that your behaviour will not harm your children. This may be unacceptable to you, and therefore difficult to deal with. The first priority is to manage the situation in order to produce the best outcome for you and your children. Your understandable feelings of outrage at the injustice could be judged negatively. Any irritability on your part might be seen as a potential risk to your children.

The other reason for co-operating fully with those who may become involved is to make sure that the process takes as short a time as possible. Make it clear that you are concerned to make progress in order to resolve matters quickly. Delay is likely to affect your children's relationship with you adversely. The younger your children are, the greater the risk of this happening. Strangely, there is an assumption that the younger they are, the less they need to see you. There is no social scientific proof that this is the case, or that one parent is less important to their development and well-being than the other. There is, however, lots of research (Part Four, No 13) that indicates that fathers have a positive impact on their children's lives.

When children have been apart from you for some time, especially if they are very young, it is common for courts to suggest a gradual build-up of parenting time. Again, it may seem unnecessary to be expected to go through this process with your children. After all, many parents, mothers *and* fathers successfully care for children.

It really may be more a question of ensuring that the other parent's insecurities, etc. are reduced. If they are anxious or uncertain, this will rub off on the children. It may therefore be better to accept what's asked of you. Or you could suggest your own parenting schedule, being mindful that the court will need to be persuaded that your first concern is for your children.

"You may want to blank the other parent out of your mind altogether."

The experience of being under suspicion can leave deep wounds. Fortunately, many FNF members are able to say that eventually, their children are free to have a more normal relationship with them. It is, however, worrying that suggestions that you may have harmed them, implanted in their minds when they were much younger, may never be quite eradicated. *'I don't want to talk about it.'* It may be a grey area that neither you nor they either choose to discuss, or feel you want to discuss.

CONTACT CENTRES

This valuable service enabled 9,761 fathers, 1,675 mothers, 655 grandparents and 469 siblings to spend valuable time with a son, daughter, grandson, granddaughter, brother or sister.

(NACCC Annual Review 2006 – 2007)

When parents cannot agree about arrangements for children they may be referred to a contact centre. Increasingly, it may be suggested as a route to break the deadlock, a halfway house to proper, independent time with children. In some cases, the court may order 'contact' to take place at a contact centre.

"Many fathers are understandably horrified at the very thought of having to meet their children under such unnatural circumstances."

It may be hard to accept this arrangement, especially when there is no good reason why you and your children should not meet in more 'normal' circumstances. Remember, if having failed to resolve arrangements for children, you are forced to ask the court to intervene, they will recommend whatever is felt to be in the children's best interest.

Contact centres provide a safe, neutral ground for children to meet their 'other' parent. If allegations of abuse of children are made, even where there is nothing to substantiate the claims, the court may decide that contact centres are a compromise, safeguarding children *should* there be any risk. For those falsely accused of whatever misconduct, this is doubly difficult.

Centres may also be used '...*where concern has been expressed about the visiting parent's ability to care for a child during contact*' (National Association of Child Contact Centres [NACCC] Part Four, No 19). It can also be a way to re-start a child/parent relationship especially where trust between the parents has broken down. It is understandable that in some circumstances, e.g. if either parent was a recovering alcoholic, some assurance would be needed that he or she could cope.

'Supported contact' and 'supervised contact'

These terms are often misunderstood, and used inaccurately. Using the wrong term may give the impression that there are established reasons why you *have* to be supervised.

Be aware that there is a significant difference between 'supported contact' (where families do not present a significant risk to a child) and 'supervised contact'. If risk is an issue, sessions will be supervised to protect the child. Those supervising (and often paid to do so) may also take formal notes during the sessions, to inform the court.

In all other situations, the term 'supported' should be used, and there is no requirement for anyone to make a formal record of what you and your child choose to do with your time together.

So what are the centres like? They are run by a variety of organisations such as church groups and the WRVS. Most are affiliated to NACCC (around 350 members throughout the British Isles, with an additional 35 supported by the Scottish Association). There is a Code of Practice, but each centre is independent.

The premises can vary from ancient church buildings to modern halls. Some have separate facilities for parents to wait whilst meetings take place, others do not. Hours vary too, limited by the premises and helpers available. Your experience therefore will depend largely on where you live, and the attitudes of those running the centre. Most centres provide a 'hand-over' service, so that parents do not have to come face to face. This does have advantages, especially limiting children's exposure to any problems between their parents.

Those working at centres are mainly volunteers. They are there to help but not interfere. They are not there to judge, or to 'take sides'. Their main concern is to provide neutral ground for the children, to minimise conflict for them if at all possible. Basically, no one likes 'having to use' a centre, but many parents have commented that they appreciate the volunteer staff are generally doing their best.

It's not ideal, you may find it humiliating, it may be said not to be 'meaningful contact', but is it better than nothing? It's impossible to forget that we have to deal with the real world, not how we know it should be. One father described what the experience was like for him. He hadn't seen his baby son for months because the mother refused to allow him to do so. 'Contact' was eventually ordered to be at a contact centre in order that father and son could get to know one another again. Dad, although disappointed and nervous said:

"I had to start somewhere, and could deal with it as long as it was only short-term. After all, if there's nothing else..."

He and his son met for an hour each week, increasing to two hours after three months. He found it difficult and stressful because the mother would stay in the room (this centre had nowhere else for mums to wait). If the baby cried, she would take him home. However, he said that the volunteers at the centre were really sympathetic to fathers, and although they couldn't interfere in any way, they did eventually persuade Mum to stay downstairs. After six months, the order was reviewed. Mum still wanted to use the contact centre, but the court ordered that Dad could take his son home. The relationship between the parents is still a problem, but he now plays a part in his son's life.

Some dads find that all does not work out quite like this, but are still prepared to do whatever it takes in the long-term interests of their children. One travels from Europe every two weeks to visit his children at a contact centre. All previous arrangements had proved so unpredictable that it seemed the better option. Approximately two-thirds of families who try contact centres move on to more 'normal' parenting afterwards. Other parents, however, are still meeting their children in this limited environment years later.

When this is happening because one parent is determined to impose conditions on the ongoing relationship between children and the other parent, life can be unpleasant for all, including the children. There will be no opportunity for anyone other than that parent to explain what is happening and why they have to meet Dad at a contact centre. Why isn't he allowed to take them outside, or worse, why can't he be trusted? NACCC has produced excellent books to help children (Part Four, No 57).

To sum up, contact centres have a part to play in helping some children. The input by the dedicated volunteer staff has to be appreciated. *If there is no viable alternative,* and your children are able to spend some time with you, this may be preferable to them not being with you at all. However, the ultimate aim must be to keep this interlude as short as possible. Children should be able to resume a more relaxed relationship with those that care for them with the minimum delay.

The following might help you decide what to do if a contact centre is proposed in your situation.

> ➢ *You may be able to convince everyone that it is not necessary. You will have to prove to the court, and especially the mother, that your intentions and behaviour are beyond reproach, and that you are capable of looking after your child. It sometimes helps if you can show you have the support of the child's grandparents.*

> ➤ *If 'supported contact' is ordered, build in a review after a short period, and/or put forward a plan to gradually move to more natural parenting over an agreed time-span. Make this part of the agreement if you can.*

It is important to be seen as willing to co-operate, but meeting at a centre should be a short-term compromise.

If you find what is suggested or ordered unacceptable, and if there is no other way to see your child, consider carefully what not agreeing to this will mean for your relationship with your child. Be warned that if the alternative is not seeing them at all, you will have little opportunity to talk to them about anything, let alone explain how much you care about them. One father sums up how he coped as follows:

"The main advice I would give any father or mother in similar circumstances is to make sure to keep up whatever little time together they can get, however difficult. The child will see this and respect them for it, and as time goes on and the child gets more and more say in his or her own life, things will gradually improve."

Children have to go along with whatever adults and the system decides for them. This does not mean that they should accept contact centres as a normal part of life. No one has yet to come up with all the answers to the problems when families break down. Given an opportunity and the approval of those around them, what would children choose? You may have limited choices too, so at least you understand how they feel.

A message from Eunice Halliday, a past director of NACCC:

"It is important for 'non resident' parents not to feel a failure because they are seeing their child at a contact centre. It is an indication of how hard they are trying to be there for their child...we know that many parents find coming to a centre a major ordeal."

If you need to, you can find contact centre locations with the NACCC website search facility (Part Four, No 19).

Think long-term

Such precautions are seldom taken in 'ordinary' families yet, despite all the mistakes made every day, children seem to survive regardless. You may therefore think that what is required of you, simply because you no longer live with the other parent, is unreasonable, and you may feel resentful. Attitudes and practices are gradually improving things for fathers but in the meantime, you have to make the best of what can seem a very poor deal.

The over-riding advice from past and present FNF membership is *be prepared to compromise in the short-term if it will help you realise your long-term aim.*

SUPPORTING CHILDREN

When children live mainly with the other parent, how do you continue to play a part in their lives? Without up-to-date information about, for example, their progress at school, health problems, or simply what interests they have, who their friends are, you will be less able to help, less involved in their lives.

If you can, come to an arrangement on sharing information with the other parent at a much earlier stage, before any contentious issues crop up.

Consider having a written agreement (Parenting Plan, p11) drawn up as proof that you both want to work together for your children's sake. It can be useful to re-focus attention on the importance of co-operation and the benefits to your children, if all does not go smoothly in the future.

If there is minimal or no communication between the two homes and no agreement, getting information may present problems. Realistically, when lives diverge to this extent, it is probably best to deal directly with those (schools, medical staff, etc.) who come into contact with your children. If handled sensitively, this can save time and avoid conflict.

Getting information about your children

If you have PR (p8), you can make independent decisions for your children when they are with you. As a parent, you should be given information that affects your children, but, following separation, you might find that you need to ask for this. How you ask can make a big difference. The lack of knowledge relating to the legal rights and responsibilities when parents no longer live together is widespread. Even if you are clear about the legal position, do not expect others either to know or understand. This can result in many situations where you are refused information about your child, or even treated as if you present a threat.

The legal position also varies across the various professional fields. It would seem logical for responsible parents to have up-to-date information about the medical condition of their children, especially young children. If you have PR you have a right under the Data Protection Act 1998 to ask for such information, and the majority of parents will be granted access to medical records. However, doctors can limit or deny access in some circumstances, e.g. if they consider the information might cause serious harm to the physical or mental health of the child (or any other person). The General Medical Council has also issued guidance about considering the wishes and feelings of young patients, according to their age and maturity (Part Four, No 14).

Increasingly, we hear that parents cannot obtain information because their child refuses to give their permission, for example, for school photos to be shared with one parent. Quite rightly, children should be involved in decisions that impact upon them, and their privacy should be respected. But throughout parental separation, are the emotions and motives of children, who may be distressed or alienated, fully understood or considered? When shouldering the responsibility for such emotionally charged decisions, children may feel confused and guilty: all the more reason for you to remain in their lives even if the going gets tough for you.

➤ *It can be frustrating to be told by a doctor that he will not let you see your child's medical records.*

➤ *It can be humiliating to be told by the school secretary that you can't speak to the child's teacher unless she checks that the other parent doesn't object.*

> ➢ *It can be alarming to be told by the hospital receptionist that they can't give you information about your child's progress because you are not the 'resident parent'.*
> ➢ *And it's heartbreaking to learn that your child doesn't want you to have copies of their school photos.*

All the above examples are common: you will have to learn to deal with this and much more. It is not a personal attack on your character. The government department responsible for schools (the Department for Children, Schools and Families [DCSF]) issues clear guidelines to schools (Part Four, No 82). These explain whom schools should involve in issues concerning a child's education. For the purposes of education legislation this includes *all natural parents*, whether married or not, anyone else who has PR for the child (providing there are no court restrictions in place), and others who have day-to-day care of a child, even though they are not the child's parent.

Schools are increasingly being guided to involve both parents, whether separated or not:

> "...where the address of a non-resident parent is unknown, tell the resident parent that the non-resident parent is entitled to be involved in their child's education and ask that information is passed on to them."
> (Extract from teachernet.gov.uk: Part Four, No 82).

This is encouraging, but still relies on one parent's willingness to take this on board. Sadly, despite these guidelines, our experience is that many may not be familiar with, or even know about this guidance (which does not yet apply to all private schools and nurseries). Don't expect practices or attitudes to change overnight. Policy guidance takes time to filter through, and you may still meet resistance. You may still be told that the school can't send you information, regular school reports, newsletters, etc. because of the extra costs.

The DCSF view has always been that both parents are entitled to receive the same information. However, is not uncommon for school information to be given to one parent only (this saves time and effort and of course conserves resources). It is unlikely that schools will want to become involved in whether the information is passed onto the other parent. If for whatever reason you do not get the information you are entitled to, or it arrives too late for you to attend school events, explain this to the school. They should arrange to send the information directly to you (unless there is a court restriction in place). They should not treat one parent more favourably, but if you can afford it, it might be helpful to provide a supply of stamped addressed envelopes. This ensures that they send you what both parents need to know.

If you have Internet access, schools are increasingly providing information electronically. Many (including private schools that do not yet have to follow the DCSF guidance) have websites listing forthcoming events such as parents' evenings. It might also be possible for you to be sent school reports, etc. by email. This reduces school costs, and extra admin.

Change of name

Some fathers seeking information about their children are concerned when they discover a different surname is being used in school records. Courts accept that surname changes are rarely in the interests of children. A child's surname is legally protected where a Residence Order is in force. Any father with PR has a right to be consulted over a change of name by deed poll. A married father can apply for a Prohibited Steps Order to prevent a change of name. An unmarried father without PR can apply for a Specific Issue Order to determine the surname by which the child should be known. Also be aware that the name of an unmarried father cannot be entered on the birth certificate without consent of the mother, unless there is a court order in force (Court Orders concerning children, p90). NB: Changes may be made after the date of publication – contact FNF for updates.

It is not uncommon for a mother to try to change a child's surname after separating from the father, particularly where the couple were not married. Following divorce, she may ask the school to change a child's name in its records, perhaps to her maiden name. There are many arguments put forward for making such changes. When a mother re-marries, she may claim that the child will benefit from changing to her new surname, because s/he will feel less 'different' especially if there are other siblings.

As said earlier, divorce affects about two in five children by the time they are sixteen. The incidence of non-married parents splitting up is even greater. Children are therefore very likely to know others whose parents have split up and re-partnered. It is not such an issue for them as it may be for adults. It is actually very important for them to be in touch with their own identity. Pressing ahead with a name change, especially if there is disagreement, may also result in them feeling confused or guilty. It can also cause problems with schools and other authorities.

DCSF guidelines advise schools to be cautious about changing names in school records, without evidence – independent of the parent seeking to make a change

– that all with PR had given their consent. This should make it simpler for all to understand the legal implications. Sadly, the guidance also infers that where a child is already known at the school by another name, it may be in the child's interests not to alter this. However, without a change in current law regarding name-changing, there is really no scope for individual interpretation, even by schools, however well intentioned motives may appear: a child's last name is his or her legal identity. Refer to FNF's website for more comprehensive information about changing names.

Even if the other parent objects, you should be kept up to date with all aspects of your children's school, including annual and other events. Ask politely for the information. If necessary, e.g. if the school secretary isn't helpful, write or make an appointment to see the headteacher. You can refer to the DCSF guidelines, but be careful how you approach this.

The emphasis should be on the benefits of your involvement for your children. 'It's my right to have this information' may just antagonise. There is a risk of upsetting your relationship with these professionals, and perhaps that between you and the other parent (which could adversely affect arrangements for children). However, persevere without becoming belligerent. It is even more important to do so if your involvement as a parent is being resisted. If you can get the school to understand the problems and to work with you, it can be one way of keeping in touch with children when all else fails. It sends out a clear message to children that 'the school' supports your role in their lives.

Clearly, in an ideal world, there should be support in place to prevent this kind of situation developing in the first place. However, many may be reluctant to get involved. To be realistic, the school's main concern is with education. As long as children appear to be OK, e.g. are not obviously showing signs of distress or physical abuse and crucially, are not presenting any behaviour problems, not too many questions will be asked about life outside school.

Open days, parents' evenings, etc.

Some parents are able to present a united front at least for school events. This is a good example for children if achievable. However, there are all kinds of issues that can lead to problems. If, for example, either or both parents find new partners, and they also want to show an interest in children's progress, the resentment can be tangible.

Again, in an ideal world all could work together, play their respective parts in the children's lives. Children are uncomfortable if adults cannot control their own negative feelings towards each other. If you think that meeting the other parent is going to be difficult especially for your children, it is better to visit school separately. If you can discuss this with the other parent, there will be fewer misunderstandings: all will understand that the arrangements are for the benefit of the children. *The children should also be involved in the discussions*, so that they can understand that you are trying to do the best for them.

Unfortunately, the 'separateness' of parents' lives after family breakdown may not be appreciated by all. To be fair, schools are on *'slippery ground'*. They have little time to grasp all the legal issues surrounding separation and children, and they neither want nor should become involved in what appears to be a 'battle' over children. Teachers may hear two different versions of events. Don't be drawn into countering petty accusations that may be made. Conducting yourself with dignity and restraint, and remaining focused on what you can do to help your children, will earn more respect.

Teachers are more used to dealing with the parent with whom the child lives most of the time, and are unlikely to question motives. They may not realise that feedback about school is not being passed to the other parent. If you still feel you cannot make headway, you can, of course, complain to a higher level, the headteacher, the governing body and so on (FNF's website includes more comprehensive information about making a complaint). Be warned though, if all develops into a war between you and the school, it may actually not help your main aim, which is of course to play a meaningful role in your child's life. Again, you are advised to be polite, but firm.

Get involved

If you can become involved with some aspect of school life, perhaps by supporting the sports teams, joining the Parent Teacher Association (PTA) to help raise funds, or becoming a school governor, you will also be seen as an 'interested parent' (this may be crucial if at some point legal proceedings become inevitable). Networking with other parents will also be helpful. Even young children will develop a social circle that can involve their parents in outings and activities – not to mention the birthday party circuit – where the children can interact and play with their friends. You can learn a great deal about what's happening at school, how your child is coping, what their interests and friends are like.

The main benefit is to your children, who will appreciate your interest. For example, if you've actually met 'Teacher' or know what the classroom looks like, where their seat, desk, whatever is, you will both be more able to talk about their school life. But if the other parent does not encourage (or discourages) your involvement, it can cause problems for all concerned.

"A father volunteered to go on a school trip with his daughter's class: extra adults were needed to supervise the children. The mother told him that if he did, she would keep the child away from school."

Irrational though this may sound (and given that the mother was a primary teacher herself), this is an example of a common dilemma. Unless you do what the other parent wants, she or he will create problems for the children, which you will be blamed for. What to do about it? There are no absolute rules, because no one wants to cause unnecessary conflict for children. However, backing off is not always the best thing for them long-term, probably only reinforcing the other parent's ability to prevent your involvement. *It is crucial to remain involved, for your children's sake.*

It can be soul destroying having to battle against such opposition, to gradually build up confidence in those who should not question your child's right to your support. Attitudes *are* changing, but it is a slow process. Much depends on the individuals you have to deal with, but it's sheer common sense to maximise support for children.

> Schools must do all they can to harness the benefits that Dads can bring to a child's education, even – and indeed *especially* – when parents are separated.
> (Rt Hon Beverley Hughes MP, Minister of State for Children, Young People and Families, 2007.)

There is a great deal of evidence that parental involvement is crucial, not only for success, but for all round personal development, including self-esteem, so don't doubt if it's worth you persevering.

It's worth considering the following sound advice and practical strategies, based on the collective experience and wisdom of those who contributed to the development of an FNF Parent Support Workshop: 'Keeping informed about your Child'.

'Knowledge + Effective Communication is Power'

Lack of knowledge is no excuse

When parents live apart, of course it's important to know the facts about rights and responsibilities regarding children. But often, knowing the 'law' is one thing; convincing those who work with your children (e.g. schools, health services) to keep you in the communication loop may not be straightforward. Many you meet may lack even basic understanding of family law as it impacts upon separated parents. And we know from experience that government guidance on these issues often goes unnoticed, buried beneath the mountains of red tape routinely received these days. Even basic terms like 'Parental Responsibility' are not widely understood. Think about it: before you separated from your partner, how much did you know about this minefield? That said, there is no excuse for anyone treating you unfairly and disrespectfully, simply because you are a 'separated' parent.

But be prepared for confusion, and having to explain the legalities as you go along, especially if the other parent is resisting your involvement with the school, etc.

Always act with good grace; be polite and courteous

It's clear that the main issue is not what you ask for, but how you ask for it. Being (and appearing) confident, yet not over-assertive can be a tall order, especially when trying to deal with separation from partners, children...

But behaving politely and being courteous is generally more effective than demanding your 'rights'. School personnel have a job to do, and a system they work within. That's not to say your requests for information, etc. are not important, especially to your child/ren. But if you don't get an immediate response, do not assume the world is against you. It's not necessarily because they're ignoring you...be patient. Give the school a reasonable opportunity to reply.

And be aware that different levels of schools have very different structures, which impact on how information is disseminated. E.g., many people find that the move from the relative informality, one class teacher of a primary school, to the more formal complexities of secondary education can be confusing for all. Find out how the new system works, and try to work with it. And remember that your child is also experiencing a major life change...give them space to find their feet, make new friends, and have new experiences.

Approach for staying informed

As soon as separation from the other parent seems likely, and especially if you are unknown to the school:

1. *Contact the school by phone or preferably letter and identify yourself as the child's caring parent.*

2. *Explain your circumstances briefly. I.e. you are/will be separated from the other parent, but are concerned to continue your involvement in your child/ren's lives and education.*

3. *Ask to arrange a meeting with the appropriate teacher/head/head of year. Bring supportive information/legal documents if appropriate. Be aware that family Court Orders can be confusing for those without legal training.*

4. *At each level/year, be prepared to repeat 1, 2 & 3.*

5. *Re your involvement in your child's education: let them know what you can offer...and say that you'll need to be kept informed of child's progress to maximise your support.*

6. *Support curricular activities and extra-curricular activities. Feed back to the teacher appropriately...let them know you're working with them.*

7. *Get involved: join the Parent Teacher Association (PTA) to help with fund-raising, etc. Consider becoming a school governor.*

8. *If this approach fails, don't take it personally. Don't lose self-esteem. Call FNF! Check the FNF website for information on how to complain.*

9. *Refer to, and refer school to the DCSF guidelines for informing parents.*

10. *Ask about the school policy on including parents (plural). This is part of their Ofsted inspection, so there should be one...*

Most important of all, throughout this process
Don't compromise your children.
Parents can be SO embarrassing!

Maintenance

Children need support (not just financial support) from their parents. This support is best provided when both parents are involved in their lives. Sharing care of children, spending time with them, gives both parents a greater understanding of their needs and an opportunity to choose appropriate essentials or presents. This is especially important when as is inevitable for many families, parents are not able to communicate, or one or both refuse to co-operate. Being instructed simply to pay up, without perhaps having a relationship, any contact with, or information about children is bound to cause resentment.

Whatever the financial arrangements for children before parents lived apart, this becomes a major issue afterwards. There is still a 'let's get the maximum out of this for our side' approach to the division of family assets. There may be precious few assets to share in some cases, increasing the pressure as living standards inevitably fall for everyone.

> ☛ "It is a fact that many 'contact' disputes are ultimately about money." ☚

If the CSA (p72) is not involved, you can both draw up your own agreement about financial responsibility for children. Include a plan for regular meetings to exchange information, and to discuss the children's changing needs. All are more likely to feel happy about expenditure if they are involved in the decisions. Unfortunately it's not always easy to reach agreement. You also need to be aware that if you do come to a 'voluntary agreement' this does not prevent later CSA involvement in some circumstances. Make the payments via a bank, and/or get receipts. Keep evidence that the money is for child support. If you do not, you could end up paying twice.

There are so many issues that can cause resentment, envy and suspicion. Children are drawn into these disputes and can have damaging examples set for their futures. Therefore, the best advice must be to consider how all this effects them. Whatever the disagreement between you and the other parent, children need protecting from the fallout.

Children under pressure

Don't be drawn into arguments about money in front of children. They will not fully understand all the complex issues involved. If for example, one parent claims the other doesn't pay, won't pay, isn't paying enough, this can lead to resentment and could seriously affect attitudes to the parent claimed to be selfish and uncaring.

> *"My dad doesn't pay my mum enough maintenance. He doesn't care about me."*

Children also dislike being used as messengers. It can be obvious that they have been rehearsed to ask you for something. It shouldn't be their responsibility. They have to face the other parent when they go home. If you don't agree to buy whatever it is, they will feel worried in case they get into trouble. *They really can't win.* It may be that you are quite happy and able to buy them whatever they have asked for, but should you just pay up? Some would advise not giving in because it encourages children to be manipulative, or to see Dad's role as just a 'cash dispenser'. Others would say pay a bit more if you can.

> *"Err on the generous side financially if it means the difference between little or no time with children and a more relaxed situation. It's amazing how much easier negotiations become when you cough up!"*

Not all parents will be able to afford to do this, especially when there are others also involved e.g. new partners, perhaps other children. It is difficult to please or be fair to everyone. Whatever your views, try not to forget how little children can do about the whole situation.

If the relationship between you and the other parent is tense, try to at least agree that it would be better for your children if you did not have to bargain in front of them. Arrange to meet if you can, to go through the issues causing concern. It may be that in your situation this is impossible. You could write explaining that you take your responsibility for your children seriously, do your best to support them, but may have different views on how to provide the support.

If you do not see your children often, and have little chance to get to know what they may need, what their interests are, it can be almost impossible for example, even to decide what would be an appropriate present. In the circumstances you may prefer to save for their future, perhaps opening a more long-term bank account for driving lessons, or further education. *Be warned that if you cannot agree on a way forward, there is a real risk that this will lead to even less time with your child.*

Responsibility

The vast majority of fathers would give their children *'the top brick off the chimney'* if they were free to do so. *Free to do so*: that's the key issue. Some fathers are not free to do so because they may be unemployed, or on low pay. Some fathers may want to support their children more freely, but are not allowed to see them often or at all.

One of the saddest developments is the numbers of young fathers being deliberately excluded from their children's lives, almost from the birth of the child. The mothers of these young men contact FNF. The whole family is desperate to love the child, even though in some cases, the young dad may not be able to offer much financial support. They are a far cry from the typical media image of 'feckless youths'. They need help to help their children. What can they do if the child's mother, often backed by her family, does not want their help (apart from maintenance, if they can afford it)?

Research has shown that fathers who spend more time with their children support them willingly: the involvement they have in their lives is a crucial factor. If you know what your children need, you will do your best to sort it out. If you know what they want, you can decide whether they should have whatever it is. It is unrealistic to expect parents no longer living together, with separate lives, perhaps new partners and children, to be able to always agree amicably about who should pay and how much for children in common. Current legislation locks such households together for a child's lifetime, encouraging envious and acquisitive attitudes that are so damaging for all concerned, especially children.

Research also shows that the majority of parents who can afford to do so, regularly and willingly pay maintenance for their children. Many pay money to the other parent even when they have a shared parenting arrangement with equal care of the children. The state formal system for assessing maintenance (following sections) has received widespread criticism from mothers and fathers since it was set up. In 2008, yet more changes were made. FNF has submitted proposals that would be fairer to both parents and, crucially, cause less conflict for children. Until these concerns are fully taken on board, the advice must be to work with what you are legally obliged to.

The following is an overview of past and current (at time of publication) maintenance regimes in the UK. Since 1993, there have been many changes. The rules are complex, made even more so by the legacy from past regimes for collecting maintenance, either through the courts or previous Child Support

Agency (CSA) policies (see next paragraphs). *Always check the latest information that applies to your family.*

Child Maintenance Enforcement Commission (CMEC)

CMEC was set up in 2008 and now has responsibility for the child maintenance system in Great Britain (Part Four, No 35). According to CMEC, the CSA will continue to assess and collect maintenance under the two old CSA schemes for the foreseeable future. It will also assess and collect maintenance where a new 'client' chooses to use the CSA system.

CMEC continues to work from the premise that children have one 'parent with care' (the recipient of maintenance) and one 'non-resident parent' (the maintenance provider). Although the CMEC rules give parents more options for deciding their own private maintenance arrangements, these will in many cases be limited for 'non-resident' parents where the other parent (or their circumstances) dictates arrangements.

Child Maintenance Options (part of CMEC) is a service set up to provide information on the options for arranging child maintenance. Their website includes an on-line calculator to work out an estimate of maintenance payments (Part Four, No 35). It also includes a form that could be used to record a private agreement. But note that this form is not a legal document. The advice is still to keep records of all payments made, whether directly to the other parent, or on maintaining the child.

Child Support Agency (CSA)

(The CSA now operates under the umbrella of CMEC)

Before 1993, if parents could not agree about maintenance for children this was largely decided by courts. In 1993, the Child Support Act 1991 saw the formation of the CSA. Parents could still make their own arrangements unless the other parent began to claim Income Support. If that happened, the CSA decided how much maintenance had to be paid. In 2003, due to almost universal discontent and pressure, radical changes were made to the CSA rules for collecting maintenance. Those involved with the CSA prior to the rule changes still pay according to the original assessment formula.

The CSA calculator gears the amount of maintenance to the average number of nights children spend with their 'non-resident' parent each year. Maintenance to be paid to the 'parent with care' is reduced, if children spend at least 104 nights with their other parent (regrettably, for those still trapped by the old rules, the number of nights is still 52). We know from the experiences of our membership that these thresholds encourage parents to reduce overnight stays in order to retain maximum maintenance. It is a fact that some solicitors advise their clients that 'allowing' children more time with their other parent can result in maintenance being reduced. This does nothing to help parents sort out arrangements for children amicably, or in the best interests of children who should be retaining a continuing relationship with both parents.

Sanctions

The CSA uses a range of sanctions to collect unpaid maintenance. These include deduction from earnings orders, liability orders, instructing bailiffs, third party debt orders, charges on property, orders for sale of property, driving licence disqualification and imprisonment. These sanctions are increasingly applied (the CSA website includes statistics).

CMEC has even great powers that can be used alongside the CSA sanctions: many can be applied without the need to apply to court for liability orders.

Proceeds from the sale of assets including houses can be seized. Information about financial affairs can be obtained directly from banks, etc., and payments and/or arrears can be taken directly from bank accounts.

A curfew, or disqualification from holding or obtaining a passport, can be imposed via a court order. Arrears can even be recovered from deceased persons' estates. More developments are underway: the government is seeking even greater enforcement powers for CMEC.

If CMEC is involved, you have no choice but to pay. Make sure you check the assessment, because, historically, many have been inaccurate. Be aware that you are liable to pay as soon as you receive their first enquiry form. This might pre-date the actual assessment when it eventually arrives. Delays or mistakes in the assessment are common and can mean huge arrears building up. If you are challenging a decision, perhaps start saving a regular sum so that when you eventually find out what you owe, you are not overwhelmed by the amount claimed. Keep records of all money paid to the other parent for children, plus any allowable expenses such as travelling to and from work.

There is not scope in this guide to cover all maintenance-related issues. If CMEC becomes involved in your child support calculations, you should get up-to-date information and advice. NACSA (National Association for Child Support Action, Part Four, No 20) may also be able to offer advice. CMEC has a comprehensive website, including a maintenance calculator. *Make sure you get the up-to-date information you need, especially as changes throughout the past years have resulted in several CSA schemes co-existing* (Part Four, No 20, 35 & 36).

As CMEC develops, the intention is that parents will have much more flexibility to make their own arrangements, and in time everyone will move onto the CMEC regime. FNF is watching this development closely, and, given the past history of the CSA, is not expecting miracles. There are major concerns about the draconian measures already being used, and the hounding of 'easy targets'. Parents who have regularly paid maintenance as agreed, are being informed that they now owe extra money. Their increased maintenance payments are being stopped directly from their wages. Querying decisions takes ages, and the grounds for appeal are limited to basic administration such as accuracy of names, addresses and National Insurance numbers. Meanwhile, the additional sums are taken regardless. Also of great concern is the tone of the information on the CMEC website, inferring that 'non-resident' parents per se seek to avoid paying maintenance.

FNF is not alone in its campaign to oppose this punitive, inflexible strategy. *Sadly, it does not yet look as if there is a grasp of the impact of these draconian measures upon the relationship between parents, families, and especially children.*

SUPPORT FROM THE WIDER FAMILY

Grandparents (and aunts, uncles, others who care)

Family breakdown also affects grandparents and other members of the family with whom children may have had regular contact. When children lose contact with one part of their family, they lose their heritage, the memories of that half of the family. A grandparent is someone they can turn to perhaps when their parents are preoccupied or unsupportive. The grandparent's home is more likely to be a haven where children are accepted without question, and where they learn more about their parents.

> "If it weren't for my grandparents I wouldn't have known who my dad was."

Where contact is lost, the outcomes for the respective families can be very different. Whichever parent is apart from children, it is likely that his or her wider family will not see children either. This is so stressful. Many grandparents in this situation are afraid they will be forgotten, even fear dying without seeing these children again. One grandfather sent a letter enclosing a photo of 'nanny and granddad' to a 'missing' grandchild asking *'Do you remember us?'* He did not get a reply. Even though grandparents may be keen to help sort out the problems, they may not know what to do for the best, and be reluctant to interfere. This quote, from an FNF support workshop for grandparents, sums up how many 'separated' grandparents feel.

"What could we do? We were powerless."

In contrast, the 'other' grandparents may find themselves playing a larger part in the children's lives. They too will offer emotional and financial support, in some cases they help by being child-minders. They may also worry about being drawn into a situation over which they have little control. The disparity between the two wider families can cause problems. It is only natural that one will feel left out, not valued. This may make communication between the two families difficult. However, although both sets of grandparents may be affected differently, they both have a practical role to play, can be a quiet voice of reason when all around are losing the plot. This can be helpful for children who find what's happening between their parents worrying. If there is still some stability, if practical solutions are put forward for resolving problems, it is a good example for everyone.

After all attempts to see his grandson had failed, a grandfather decided to write to the other grandparents. It was not an easy decision for him because the two families had not spoken since their children divorced years earlier. The other grandparents didn't write back, but soon after, the daughter-in-law rang to say she was bringing their grandchild to see them. The advice to grandparents is much the same as that to fathers:

> ➤ *Don't make assumptions.*
> ➤ *Don't be discouraged: make opportunities to keep in contact.*

Perhaps your grandchildren don't visit anymore, or you feel you may not be welcomed by the other parent. It takes a great deal of courage to face possible rejection, but crucially, the children need to know that you still love them regardless of changes to the family situation. Send letters, cards, make phone calls, even if there is no response. It is important for the children to know you are still there, even if out of sight.

Just how *do* children make sense of what is happening? They are relatively powerless too, and shouldn't feel guilty for something they cannot control. They may not be old enough to travel alone, cannot make decisions about visiting their 'other' family. If they know that one parent does not support them seeing you, they may not even feel free to show that they would like to see you. They risk disapproval and arguments if they make a fuss, and will choose the easy route. It's really not their fault. So, the adults must help them by reaching in to their lives to say: *'Its OK, we know you still love us, and we will always love you, no matter what.'*

In fact, children may want to tell you they love you too. Some are now reaching out to their 'lost' family via the Internet. But understandably, they don't want their other parent to know this; another example of the dilemma they face.

Following separation, it can take years to understand more fully why life can become so complex and irrational, and to perhaps be clearer about the motives and weaknesses of all concerned. The following is a message of encouragement from the Grandparents' Association:

"Grandparents' Association often receives letters saying that they are now in contact with grandchildren after many years – so don't give up."

If you are not able to see your grandchildren, the Grandparents' Association may be able to advise on the way forward (Part Four, No 16). Grandparents can apply for a Contact Order (and possibly other court orders) if they obtain permission from the court. Whilst in practice such applications are often best made by the child's parent, there are cases where separate applications may be appropriate and possibly successful.

New partners

"My child is now calling someone else Daddy."

Discovering this strikes at the heart of the relationship between parents and children; it is threatening and stressful. It is normal to feel both angry and powerless, especially if your children spend limited or no time with you.

Children, even young ones, understand who their 'real' parents are. The strain of having to conform to whatever adults think they should call everyone can be a real problem for them, especially if they know they are upsetting one parent or the other. Ideally, all the adults involved should get together, to focus on what's best for children. They will need help to understand where everybody fits into the scheme of things, how each person can play a complementary but different role in their lives. The focus should be on what is best for the children (i.e. what the children are comfortable with), not what the adults find expedient.

Such co-operation and child-centredness is unfortunately not always possible. The family regarded as the 'main' family will undoubtedly make most of the decisions. You may have different views, but your children need to get by in that family, and they will only do so by fitting in, adapting to their different circumstances. This is not being disloyal, and it does not mean they love you any less. You are their parent, why would they? *Nothing, not even calling someone else 'Dad', however painful that may be for you, can change the special link your children have with you.*

"She's not his mother."

It doesn't matter at what stage you meet a new partner, he or she may present quite a problem to your children, especially if the other parent is resentful. Even when arrangements for sharing the care of children have been working reasonably smoothly for a good while, the routine is almost guaranteed to be upset. Children can feel jealous, left out, in second place. *Make sure they can spend some time just with you.* It is always difficult to balance your loyalties to all concerned. You are after all, 'allowed' a new relationship, and your children must be helped to understand this.

Advice for new partners:

> "Keep a distance from the kids, don't rush at them; try not to be too friendly. Let the children come to you. Their most likely reaction is 'Gawd….what's Dad (Mum) brought home?!' They are likely to be wary for a considerable time. Be studiously neutral about the 'old' one, and try not to replace him or her."

Again, if there is any way for all of you eventually to come together to discuss your respective roles in the children's lives, it may make a considerable difference to future relationships. An irrational dislike of the person now sharing the ex-partner's life can lead to all kinds of negativity and unfounded suspicions. If these feelings are never aired, the assumptions just get more absurd, and the misinterpretation of motives (especially concerning financial matters) can make life really difficult.

The other parent will need reassurance. They may be behaving aggressively, perhaps making it difficult for children to make contact. It takes a great deal of courage to make the first conciliatory move especially if you expect a rejection. If you can find a way to say that you still love the children, still intend to do all you can for them, it may make all the difference. Most important of all, you should all accept that you and your new partner want to share in their care, not take them away altogether.

Social attitudes *are* gradually changing as more and more fathers make it clear they don't just want to play a minor role in their children's lives. Despite this, after family breakdown it is still far more common for it to be assumed that children will live mainly with one parent (almost always the mother) and 'visit' the other parent. When a new partner moves in with a 'resident' mother, it may be claimed that the new 'family' will be disrupted if children continue to see their other natural parent. This fails to consider the effects upon children who would be faced with the prospect of having to give up a loved and loving parent. Undoubtedly there are many excellent step-parents, but the relationship between children and a step-parent can be difficult to negotiate. Divided loyalties can cause problems for all involved. Children may need extra support as they adjust to family changes, and at such times, it is even more important to preserve the stable relationship they have with you.

If you can, talk things through with your children, especially when changes are likely. This helps them to get a balanced view of what's happening. If you are lucky, they may share their own feelings and views with you too. You may be surprised how different their needs are to yours, and these must be considered. *Be aware that they will not want anything shared in confidence to rebound on them.*

Even if you find you cannot overcome resistance to others who play a part in their lives, children should not feel they have to take sides. They must learn to move forward, to form new relationships. They need your help and encouragement to be able to do this. It is so easy to be critical without good reason. You must of course speak out if there are serious concerns about their welfare. Otherwise, *they should be free to benefit from both their family environments.*

IMPLACABLE HOSTILITY

All the advice so far about being positive, behaving reasonably, etc. works from the assumption that if you work hard enough, if you genuinely try to put your children's interests first, all will be fine.

In many cases, it is not fine. The attitudes and behaviour of some parents *is* hostile and negative, and they deliberately resist the other parent's involvement to greater or lesser degrees. It may be purely a question of personality and it is unlikely that personality will change. Undoubtedly, there are families where all possible avenues have been explored, and there is no reciprocal desire to co-operate.

Children growing up under such pressure are doubly at risk. They feel stressed by the conflict that inevitably happens whenever Mum and Dad meet or speak on the phone, etc. They also have to live with the knowledge that the parent with whom they live doesn't want them to see their other parent.

It is a Catch 22 situation for them. Even though they love both parents, they are not free to show their feelings. One parent may appear angry, upset, not speak to them if they mention or visit the other parent. The guilt must be overwhelming. Many side with the parent with whom they must survive (Parental alienation, p82). They are also powerless to influence what's happening, may feel guilty because they cannot prevent it.

"I couldn't do anything about it: I was only eight at the time."

This was a comment from a child who hadn't seen one of his parents for years, after a total and sudden withdrawal of all 'contact'. Ironically, the legal advice to the father at the time was:

"Given the intransigent attitude of the mother, no court will enforce your contact order."

So it seems that the court was also powerless (or unwilling) to stop this happening (at least that's what the solicitor advised). The father therefore decided to withdraw from the 'battle' because he thought it would spare the child unnecessary distress. Plainly, conflict at the time was reduced, but at the expense of their relationship: years later they do not know one another. It's easy to be discouraged by negative or cynical advice and understandable to be worried by threats to reduce or deny your involvement as a parent. Don't be persuaded that giving up is in the interests of children, or that taking legal action is pointless. Much will depend on the court, the judge or magistrates (Using 'the system', p105). Courts are more willing to act these days, but still not willing enough.

If your child is being denied time with you, first try to establish the underlying reasons. Suggest using a mediation service (p10). Without clearing up any misunderstandings, there is less chance of resolving the situation quickly and amicably. If all attempts to reason fail, taking legal action is an obvious step when communication breaks down. Take action swiftly to prevent further damage to the relationship that has been suspended. It is a great pity that there are still no informal yet effective mechanisms in place to solve this kind of resistance without recourse to formal and costly legal proceedings. Sometimes court applications can spread out over many months, possibly years.

> *Even when the other parent's intransigent attitude is really obvious, and previous court orders have been blatantly broken, you may find that although some judges will take the robust action needed to support your child's right to a relationship with both parents, many will not: judgements across the country are inconsistent.*

During lengthy proceedings, when a 'Contact Order' continues to be ignored, this further erodes the parent/child relationship. The longer you hesitate, the more likely it is that the other parent will establish a routine for the child that doesn't include you. The courts and those who become involved may be reluctant to upset this pattern. Your determination to continue to be involved may be viewed as a threat to the children's stable life elsewhere, as in the following quote:

"I went through the whole court process over twenty times. I was always being awarded time with my child, but hardly ever saw him. I asked for the Contact Order to be enforced and was told that 'no judge in his right mind' would use the sanctions available."

In reality, very difficult choices have to be made when considering outcomes for children. Again, if you can get all to *focus on the importance for the children of a continuing relationship with* **both** *parents*, they may be more prepared to deal more firmly with the parent who is preventing your involvement. Often, your intentions are misjudged, and you will be seen as 'wanting to exercise your rights' over your children. *It may be worth emphasising that your primary concern is to meet your children's need for maximum support from family and friends.*

Many men may feel uncomfortable seeking help with private family matters, but it *is* worth contacting agencies that can mediate between you and the other parent. Never assume that your ex-partner will not co-operate. Sometimes an approach by a third party works, and can open up new channels of communication, suggest different ways forward. It has to be said that if the other parent is determined to cut you out, they may resist attempts to find a compromise, because they know this will inevitably mean they will have to 'give up' the children.

The good news is that there is some progress: the Children and Adoption Act 2006 (p108) gives courts a wider range of down-to-earth sanctions to tackle behaviour that denies children their right to be part of both parents' lives. It is too early to judge whether these measures will deal effectively with parents (mothers and/or fathers) unable to put their children's interests before their own. However, a significant step forward was made by the Midland Region Family Judges and Magistrates, who published *What the Family Courts expect from Parents*, a guide for parents seeking court orders for children (Part Four, No 85). If this no-nonsense, clear direction that children need both parents is followed, and sanctions applied where necessary, separating families will be left in no doubt about their joint responsibilities to children.

If you exhaust all avenues, but your children still lose contact with you, *you must not give up hope that, later on, things might improve. This has been the experience of so many families.* Meantime, keep records of what you tried to do to resolve the problems, to keep in touch. Include all the positive measures you took, the reasons why your attempts to stay in contact with them didn't work out. There's no need to be overly critical about the other parent. Be honest but stick to the facts. In time, everyone needs more information about the past. Those with only one part of their history will need to balance this out eventually with the other perspectives.

Parental alienation

There is a growing awareness that one parent determined to severe all contact between children and the other parent may begin to alienate children against that parent and also the wider family and friends. In extreme cases this will result in children effectively rejecting part of their family (Parental Alienation Syndrome or PAS).

This is also the territory of false accusations, used sometimes to support claims that children are afraid, do not want to see one of their parents (and/or wider family).

"I wrote to my daughter often weekly, never less than twice a month, and I sent her presents continually, not only at birthday and Christmas-times. But I very rarely got any reply. Sometimes my letters and presents were returned unopened. When my daughter did write it was hate-mail, urging me to 'go away and leave her/them alone'. Once or twice my daughter left hate-messages on my answering machine."

This is heartrendingly difficult to cope with. Many dads (and mums) in this situation refuse to give up, despite the sometimes overwhelming obstacles, especially doubts about whether their children really have stopped loving them.

Don't let others, including, sadly, the practitioners who may get involved, persuade you to back off. When faced with these intractable situations, they may be afraid to challenge the behaviour of the 'main' parent, arguing that this might cause problems for children. The easiest option will usually be to recommend that they remain with the alienating parent, even though this continues to jeopardise their relationship with the other parent. Although the term 'PAS' is widely recognised especially in the USA, you may find its use in UK courts can antagonise, especially if you are representing yourself. If describing alienating behaviour, it may be better to use more familiar terms such as brainwashing, or attempts to influence children against you.

Fortunately, there are some experts who specialise in this field, who appreciate that parental alienation is deeply damaging for children and should be dealt with accordingly. FNF may also be able to steer you in the direction of sympathetic legal and specialist advice. It also produces a comprehensive guide to parental alienation and has extensive references to related literature on its website (also see *Divorce Poison*, Part Four, No 61).

Sadly, there are many fathers (and some mothers) living apart from children who know that their children are being turned against them. If you are fearful that your child has been misinformed about you, rather than focusing on the worst that may happen, go back over the earlier advice, and try to stay positive, never give up hope for change in the future. *Above all, always remember how important it is for them to know that you love them.*

➢ *Don't assume they believe you don't care.*

➢ *Don't assume they want to believe this.*

➢ *Don't assume even if they appear to be alienated at the moment that this cannot change.*

➢ *Don't assume they are part of any attempts to discredit you. Remember they are half of you: what would they gain?*

> *In normal circumstances, children will not choose to reject a parent completely.*

Perhaps the following thoughts might persuade alienating parents that indeed they do have much to lose in the long run, if they will not let their children go, or do not realise the damage they are doing.

Children, free to love both parents, not pressured to choose between them will be less likely to resent either parent when they are mature enough to make sense of their family situation. Don't lie to your children, or deceive them. Don't encourage them to do the same. Lies are unsustainable. Sometimes years later, the missing pieces will be put together: *'That's not what I was told: is that true?*

Finding out that one parent had lied about the motives of the other, had said they didn't care when in fact they cared a great deal, is inexcusable, and may result in rejection of the deceiving parent. It doesn't matter what the reasons may have been, or how behaviour was justified. Nothing can excuse the long-term damage to a child's self-image. *When it is suspected that they are being alienated against their 'other' parent, children undoubtedly need professional help without delay.*

This section ends with one father's suggestions for making the best of a difficult situation.

"Never miss out on time with your child. Never miss a phone call or be late if you can help it. It is easy to be furious with the court for stopping you from writing more than one letter per week, and then six months later to not even keep up the one letter you are allowed. This is hard if the conditions are made awkward – e.g. only allowed to phone on Tuesdays between six p.m. and six-thirty p.m. – but you just have to do it.

"I think of ways in which you can make the best of what little contact you have got, e.g. for young children, put stickers on the outside of the envelope so they look out for letters from you. Write your letters with coloured pens, or use a coloured printer to print different colours and big print. Include clip art and pictures from the Internet. For older children, make sure you have a good website, so that they learn something about you from the pictures. There are lots of other ideas.

"Be prepared to be a doormat for the sake of your children. Just bide your time, resist all provocation and don't complain. They'll see the way that you are being treated and that it isn't your fault. Keep up some kind of contact and as they get older and more independent they'll make sure that they get more. You'll miss out on their childhood, which is a great shame, but it can't be helped."

PART THREE: Basic information

LEGAL FRAMEWORK

This section gives a general overview only and should not be regarded as a comprehensive or authoritative statement of the law. Also, law in this area is subject to change. FNF cannot be held responsible if changes to the law outdate this publication.

There are several key pieces of legislation concerned with divorce/separation and how all affects children and families. It would be helpful to familiarise yourself with these Acts, even if you are fortunate enough to sort out your arrangements relatively smoothly. The government departments that have responsibility for providing services for families produce a wide range of publications on all aspects of the law, policies and practices that may affect you. For the more detailed information you will need, start with the FNF website (and see Part Four).

It is essential to get to grips with the basic principles in the legislation. These will affect how decisions are made about your family. The following is a brief outline, not a statement of the Law.

➤ All work from the fundamental principle that the welfare of children is *paramount*, i.e. must take first priority (but is not the only consideration).

➤ If the relationship between parents breaks down, it is considered best for children to have a continuing relationship with both parents and wider family.

➤ An integral part of most legislation is the belief that arrangements decided between the parents are preferable .

➤ All should be settled as quickly as possible, because delay is seen as harmful for children.

Court Orders concerning children

(Law and practices in Scotland, N. Ireland and the Channel Islands may be different in some respects. Refer to FNF's website, and contact local branches for information.)

If parents cannot agree about arrangements after separation or divorce, a range of court orders can be applied for. The most common orders are made under the *Children Act 1989* (and subsequent amendments). The court will not make an order unless they think it will be better for children if they do (known as the 'No Order' principle).

A **Residence Order** says with whom (but not usually where) the child should live. It can be made in favour of more than one person (**Shared Residence Order or SRO**). The Children Act states that each parent retains parental responsibility after divorce and each may act independently of the other regardless of residence. SROs are usually made to stress the equality of both parents' role in children's lives. They do not necessarily define time to be spent in each home (although they may do so).

A **Contact Order** tells the person with day-to-day care of the child to 'allow contact' between the child and the person named in the order. It should be carefully drafted to include details such as times, places and conditions. This can remove any misunderstandings if conflict is anticipated. If there is goodwill between parents, they can agree to vary the order.

The court is able to make orders which require specific actions (**Specific Issue Order**) to be taken or which prohibit certain steps (**Prohibited Steps Order**) being taken in respect of children. These orders are intended to safeguard the interests of the children where major issues of concern may arise and are not intended for trivial disputes.

The Children Act also covers **Parental Responsibility Orders** and 'public' law. Be aware of the difference between *private* and *public* family law. If you have to apply to court for anything concerned with divorce, separation, and arrangements for children, this is usually 'private' law. If there are reasons why the local authorities need to get involved, e.g. if there has to be an investigation by social services, because children are thought to be at risk, this is, or may become public law.

There is a series of guides designed to help with applications to court. You can download these (and the forms needed) from the Internet (Part Four, No 43), or get them from your local civil (i.e. not criminal) court (Types of court, p95). Making an application for an order is fairly straightforward if you get the information you need (start with FNF's website).

As with all other aspects, the helpfulness or otherwise of the court in providing these guides depends to a large extent on the individual you ask. Sadly, sometimes even the staff in the courts aren't up-to-date. Don't be put off. The guides are essential reading, explaining many of the terms used in the Children Act, the orders available and what they are for, and clearly show who can apply for them. They also answer some commonly asked questions, so it's worth persevering.

Common practice

Although all is geared to *'the best interests of children'*, there are no hard and fast rules governing what this actually means. It therefore becomes a matter for individual interpretation. When making decisions courts will also refer back to past court judgements (case law: Part Four, No 6). In practice, delays are commonplace; applications are not necessarily simple. Some require many appearances in court. Where there are real differences between parents, the process can stretch over many years, and still not resolve matters satisfactorily. Of greater concern, when the first edition of this book was published, was that current outcomes did not adequately reflect or encourage the Children Act 1989 principle that children should have a continuing relationship with both parents (and wider family), wherever possible. Extensive government consultations since then have resulted in some progress towards an acknowledgement that denying a child this right to know their family is harmful. Courts now have additional sanctions (e.g. community service orders) to use when one parent refuses to share care of children for no good reason. It is too early to tell whether, in practice, this will more fully protect children's relationships with both parents.

Whatever your future involvement with the family justice system, if you eventually decide you may have to apply for a court order concerning your children, a working knowledge of the basic principles gives you a greater chance of understanding your options, and intelligently instructing your solicitor (also see 'Representing yourself', p98).

The cost of employing a lawyer to conduct your case is high, and the courts are under pressure to reduce the burden on the taxpayer – it is estimated that public expenditure related to family breakdown adds up to billions of pounds each year.

Other than those on benefits, few fathers qualify for assistance with legal costs, and this has led to a growing number representing themselves in court – they simply have no choice. For those who qualify for legal aid, the choice of solicitors is limited and the service can be rudimentary, but not everyone is confident enough to represent themselves. Many parents still seek the help of a solicitor, with mixed success (see 'Choosing a solicitor', p95).

The provision of legal aid is another area that has undergone substantial change. The Community Legal Service (CLS: Part Four, No 34) funds legal aid.

Family mediation is encouraged to resolve disputes when couples split up. Those eligible for legal aid are required to have a meeting with a mediator to assess whether mediation is suitable for them. There are exceptions, for example, in cases of domestic abuse, where the travel time is too great, and where the other parent will not consider mediation (the CLS website includes funding criteria).

Research by the National Audit Office (2007) showed that mediation reduced both costs and time to reach agreement. However, only twenty per cent of people funded for family breakdown cases tried mediation. Some were not told about this option by their legal representative. The ongoing advice in this book is not to rely on one source of information, even a solicitor or court staff. Search through FNF's comprehensive website to check the facts. The Community Legal Service was launched in April 2000, intended to make it easier to resolve disputes by providing public access to legal information at libraries, law centres, Citizens Advice Bureaux (Part Four, No 8) and via the Internet.

UNDERSTANDING THE SYSTEM

"At the time of my divorce, I was at a complete loss what to do when I had hardly any contact with my children during the first three months. I found out about FNF by an opportune item on the Radio."

If you decide or have no choice about legal action, the following is an overview of the 'family justice system', to familiarise you with some of the lessons learned by others, sometimes at great cost to their families.

Getting the right information can be the key to making positive decisions. The family justice system can be very confusing. You will need to find out as much as you can about how it operates, the language used, and the professionals you may meet, as early as possible. *If you need information, don't be afraid or embarrassed to ask for it.* If the first person you speak to isn't helpful, ask someone else. If you are not sure what's happening, who people are, find out. It's your family, although sometimes it may seem that everybody else appears to know more about it than you do! Because they work in the court situation day in, day out, they may forget that not everyone is as 'at home' as they are. They also forget that jargon they use all the time may be like a foreign language to you. You need to make sense of it: ask for an explanation if you don't understand.

The following is only a brief introduction to some of the services that may become involved with your family as you divorce or separate from your partner. FNF produces comprehensive guides to some of these services (details in Part Four). Also note that there will be differences in Scotland and N Ireland. Contact local FNF groups in those areas.

A reflection of membership feedback:

> *"Exhaust all the other options before going to court. Find a more constructive forum to allow the children's needs to be given priority."*

> *"Once an application to the court has been made, you must wholeheartedly see it through, unless better alternatives present themselves. Too many fathers, especially the best and most decent among them, give up because it seems too painful for all concerned. This short-term reduction in stress can mean a long-term loss for children."*

The Family Court

Many families fail to reach agreement, for all kinds of reasons. If after exploring all other ways to sort out arrangements you still cannot agree, you may have to take legal action. To repeat earlier advice, it is crucial that you act swiftly if the contact between your children and yourself is stopped or is resisted, because delay can damage both your relationship with them, and your chances of reinstating the time they spend with you.

> If you do decide to apply for an order, you should still continue 'parallel' attempts to reach agreement with the other parent. Always remember that once the court or other professionals become involved, they have extensive powers and discretion to make decisions for your family.

Be aware that going to court is not straightforward. There are no easy solutions when parents cannot agree. Don't assume that the court is any better at finding 'the answer' to your problems. Don't assume that they will be interested in being 'fair' to you or the other parent.

Everything presented to the court should be considered in relation to how it affects your children. A decision will then be made based on what is thought to be the best course of action for children (note: not the parents). Be prepared to prove you put your children's interests first. If you feel they would benefit from more time with you, ask for regular reviews. Draw up a Parenting Plan (p11) detailing how your children's time can be shared between you and the other parent. This will show you have thought things through. If at all possible, work on this with the other parent.

You may find that the whole court experience is very different from what you expect, and the outcome not what you had hoped for.

"I represented myself in my own case, and am a frequent McKenzie (p98) for others and I can say that the only predictable thing is that the outcome is unpredictable!"

It is common to have to make more than one application. Don't expect the court to settle everything finally: situations and people change. Court orders may define some things, but cannot cover everything. If problems arise, you may need to make further applications at any time.

Types of courts

It makes life more confusing to discover that there are different types and levels of courts that deal with family matters, as follows:

- ☞ High Court *(London): the case is likely to be heard by more experienced senior judges.*
- ☞ County Courts: *where a district or circuit judge will hear the case.*
- ☞ Family Proceedings Courts: *usually consisting of a bench of lay magistrates guided by a court clerk.*

Most applications can be made in either of the last two courts, but certain applications (including the more 'difficult' cases) are made direct to the High Court. Family cases in England and Wales are heard 'in private' with the press and public excluded, so you will not be able to observe other cases. The *Appeal Court* (London) deals with appeals against earlier court rulings (members of the public are usually admitted to this court). Note that as from April 09, appeals from a Magistrates Court are heard by the County Court. Also note that moves are afoot to improve the openness of the family courts, but it isn't yet clear how this will work in practice, or how it will impact upon judicial decisions.

To add to this confusion, we know that courts also vary from area to area; each area has developed a slightly different ethos. Also, within individual courts, different judges may have very different views. This can and does impact on outcomes for families, making it difficult to give general advice. If at all possible, speak to others who have local knowledge. You could visit a local FNF meeting, or join the FNF members' only Internet discussion groups (FNF Self-Help and FNF Chat: Part Four, p117).

Choosing a solicitor

Most people think that they must go to a solicitor when faced with decisions about separating from their partner. However, this could be a big and expensive mistake. If you decide you cannot manage without professional help, *be warned, not all solicitors can 'do your divorce' for you.* You will need one that specialises in family law.

Some legal practices are affiliated to 'Resolution' (previously known as the Solicitors Family Law Association [SFLA]), whose Code of Conduct recommends handling family cases in a manner which minimises conflict, especially for children (Part Four, No 24). In our experience, this does not always guarantee good service or ensure that the outcome for your family will be any better. Many FNF members lose confidence in solicitors, even well-known, expensive ones. Lawyers will tell you 'A fool is his own lawyer', but some members will tell you quite the opposite (Representing yourself, p98). As with all things, the quality and type of service you will pay for varies enormously, and many are dissatisfied with their lawyers. Much depends on the individual who eventually takes on your case. It takes talent and years of experience to be a good family lawyer. They do exist, but finding the right one to represent you may not be straightforward. Recommendations, even by other FNF members may not be enough: what suits one family may be inappropriate for another.

It is a bit of a minefield, and the unwary should read the FNF guide to choosing and using a solicitor (Part Four, p118: available from the FNF Office or website). Even if desperate for legal advice, always find out as much as you can before making a decision.

More advice from members:

> "You must instruct legal representatives to act as you want them to. You know the case better than they do. Don't let them sell you short. They may try to persuade you that the best you can hope for is the 'normal' outcome, i.e. one 'resident' parent. Accept this and you become the 'visiting' parent. There are other arrangements that enable children to benefit more easily from the support of both parents."

> "Shared parenting should be the norm, and enforced, so that children can gain love and support from both parents and the wider family."

It must be borne in mind that there may be greater awareness of alternative outcomes, but courts change slowly, and are very conservative. Professional advice may be based on experience of what is a likely outcome (i.e. children will live with one parent, usually the mother). Anyone substantially disagreeing with 'the experts' may be perceived as 'being unreasonable', may even end up with getting less than the 'norm'. It is a dilemma: only you can decide what seems to be the best way forward for you and your family. FNF's statements on shared parenting are essential reading (FNF booklets: Part Four, p118).

Beware of legal costs

It is quite easy to rapidly rack up a huge legal bill: tens of thousands of pounds are not uncommon, even where things are fairly straightforward. Disputes about financial matters are usually the most expensive. Many solicitors are less than candid about the running costs of the case. Remember that they charge for time taken to do anything connected with your case. That includes answering telephone calls, photocopying, etc., as well as writing letters on your behalf, giving advice or acting for you in court. It also includes the whole conversation with you, so cut through the social niceties as quickly as possible and get down to business. It's essential to establish what rate per hour will be charged: it shows you will be keeping an eye on costs. Don't be afraid to negotiate on fees quoted; there is always room for manoeuvre if you ask.

> ➤ Take a list of all addresses, and anything else that otherwise might have to be recorded at the appointment.
> ➤ Before you go, make a list of what you want to deal with and take it with you.
> ➤ Ask advice on the best way to proceed, based on the list.
> ➤ Leave as soon as you have got the advice you needed, and have instructed accordingly.
> ➤ Make sure you are given draft copies of any letters so you can approve them *before* they are sent.
> ➤ Remember that it's *your* case. It's surprising how much paperwork can be generated: ask for copies and organise in a file.

If you apply for legal aid, your solicitor will be unlikely to do anything more than offer a brief consultation (and perhaps write a letter) until your entitlement is decided, and this can cause delay. Ask how long it will take and check progress if necessary. If you do qualify you should be aware that you may still have to pay part of the costs of the case.

Don't be embarrassed to follow this advice: others have learned the hard way that legal costs can be ruinous, for them and for their families. Most important of all, if you have to employ a solicitor, remember that they charge a great deal for their time and services, *whatever the outcome of your case*.

Representing yourself and 'McKenzie friends'

FNF members often choose to represent themselves in court. They may not be eligible for legal aid, but still cannot afford the huge legal costs that can mount up. Many do so because they believe it to be more effective, particularly if only one issue is involved. (Also read FNF leaflet 'Representing Yourself' – not everyone is suited to conducting their own case.)

The procedures both inside and outside the courtroom will be unfamiliar. The legal jargon used also makes it difficult to follow what is happening. It makes sense to read up on what's likely to happen beforehand. Family proceedings are generally conducted with less formality than criminal cases. As long as you are polite and respectful (and do not waste time) you need not worry too much about procedural matters. It should not be assumed that a 'Litigant in Person' (LIP) knows the rules inside out, and the court and the opposition's legal representative (if any) have a duty to explain points of law to you.

Some FNF members may be able to advise informally on how best to prepare a case and conduct yourself in court. For many years, members have acted as 'McKenzie friends' in the courtroom. It can be extremely helpful to have both practical and moral support from someone that 'knows the ropes' and more importantly, is there to help *you*, not simply to do a job.

> **PLEASE NOTE: 'McKenzie friending' is not a service run or vetted by the charity FNF. Although you may find a McKenzie friend via FNF's network of members, they work independently of FNF. The charity can neither recommend individuals, vouch for their ability or experience, nor take any responsibility for how they work with and for you. If you ask someone to act as McKenzie friend, it is up to you to check their experience, and how they can help you, and if they charge for this service (see the end of this section).**

A McKenzie friend *should* be able to go into the court with you. Although not usually allowed to address the court, they can take notes, keep you organised, and if they have sufficient knowledge, they may be able to quietly make suggestions and offer advice. Perhaps as important, afterwards, they may help you make sense of what has happened. It is easy to miss vital bits of information when nervous or uncertain. Unfortunately, despite clear guidance to judges to allow McKenzie friends, it is still not uncommon for individual courts and judges to decide whether you will be allowed this help. This varies across the country and cannot be predicted, as the following shows:

"At the door of the court the 'friend' who was with me to provide support, was refused entry by the usher, with the words 'we don't like McKenzie friends here – Mr (Smith) has no need to have a McKenzie friend'. It is impossible to predict, before appearing at the door of the court, whether such a person will be admitted."

2008 guidance from the President of the Family Division has since clarified this situation. **Make sure you read this** (Part Four, No 43). The guidance makes it clear that there is a strong presumption in favour of enabling an LIP to be assisted by a McKenzie friend. However, the LIP retains responsibility for his or her case.

In order to avoid last-minute confusion and possible disappointment, it is becoming good practice to provide the court with advance notice that you request the help of a McKenzie friend. Include their name, and brief overview of how they will be assisting. Also mention that they are aware that currently, family cases concerning children are held in private, and court rules govern publishing or disclosure of confidential, sensitive information outside the courtroom (more information: HM Court Service guidance leaflet EX710 – Part Four, No 43.

Usually, but not always, court staff are helpful to LIPs. Be warned that experienced lawyers are more familiar with the court procedures. They know what is likely to happen, what the choices might be. Some are not beyond trying to intimidate or bully you. If you cannot keep your cool (and remember emotional involvement can make this difficult), even with a McKenzie friend to support you, self-representation is probably not for you.

You must be properly prepared, and stick to the point. Your personal knowledge of the case is certain to be far greater than that of any lawyer. Therefore don't be put off by those that counsel all is doom and gloom, you have no chance of success, you'll be eaten by the barrister on the other 'side'. If you have thought through what you will say to convince the court you are more than willing and able to take responsibility for your child, and welcome being actively involved in his or her upbringing, what better argument is there? Your trump card is your honesty, decency and, above all, your love for your child. Your level of educational attainment or grasp of the law shouldn't come into it.

"A reasonable case presented reasonably has a good chance of success."

One last reminder: you may be so wrapped up in your own case that you completely forget to thank your McKenzie friend. It is also customary to pay his (or her) expenses such as travel, meals, telephone and printing costs. The FNF website includes a guide to work out these costs.

The number of people now seeking help with their court cases is growing. Changes to the legal aid system will mean reduced availability, and result in more people having to represent themselves. Volunteer (and unpaid) McKenzie friends are in short supply. The past years have seen a rise in the number of people (and organisations) offering to act as paid McKenzie friends.

With varying experience, each McKenzie friend will also have a different style and approach. This will need to match your own views on how to move forward. It's your family, not theirs. Don't be browbeaten into a decision or course of action you do not feel comfortable with.

If you are paying someone to McKenzie for you, it's also important to have a clear understanding and agreement on costs involved, *before* you ask them to work for you. E.g. receiving an unexpected and costly bill for say, telephone conversations that you thought were informal, would be quite a blow. *Again please note that McKenzie friends work independently of FNF.*

One last thought: you might like to offer to be a McKenzie friend. Acting as a McKenzie friend for someone else is a good way to gain experience for your own application.

FNF has produced a support pack for LIPs: *Give 'Em Some LIP!*, available via the FNF National Office or website (p118). Also contact FNF for information about LIP training workshops.

Cafcass (Children and Family Court Advisory Support Service)

(England and Wales only)

When the first edition of this book was compiled the services that worked within family courts were being re-organised, and Cafcass grew out of this process. Cafcass comes under the umbrella of the Department for Children, Schools and Families (DCSF), but works independently. Set up in 2001, it has undergone many teething problems, and continues to develop policies and working practices to reflect legal changes and government strategies. The overall impression at the time this second edition is published is that the ethos of this service seems to be more respectful of the families and children it works with. Crucially, a transparent inspection process (by Ofsted: Part Four, No 48) is now in place. But as said in the author's note, and judging by the experiences of those who contact FNF, vestiges of out-dated and unhelpful practices and attitudes linger. It may take a while for this service to provide the kind of consistent, down-to-earth support that separating families need to ensure children get the best of both parents' worlds, but we are hopeful...and again, we will be watching...

This is THE pivotal service that may become involved in decisions that are made for your family, especially if you cannot agree about arrangements for your children.

It is crucial to get a grasp of who they are, what they do, and even more important, where they fit into the family justice system.

It is unlikely that you will have a clear idea about what Cafcass does.

"Our role is to:

➢ Safeguard and promote the welfare of children
➢ Give advice to the family courts
➢ Make provision for children to be represented
➢ Provide information, advice and support to children and their families."

(Cafcass website)

When parents who are separating or divorcing can't agree on arrangements for their children, and make an application to court (private law: see p90), Cafcass officers act as Children and Family Reporters (CFRs) or if children need to be represented separately, they act as Guardians ad Litem (GALs). You may find that many people simply refer to them as 'Cafcass officers'; therefore, in the following section this is the term that will be used, or just 'officer'.

After you make an application for a court order, a Cafcass officer will usually be appointed. A Dispute Resolution appointment with the officer is a preliminary meeting at court to help families try to resolve any disputes about arrangements for children. Cafcass claims that nearly sixty per cent of these early interventions result in full or partial agreements at the first court hearing. This hearing is when the court will decide what should happen next. The officer might also be asked to write a welfare report for the court.

If attempts to reach agreement are unsuccessful, Cafcass officers are charged with finding out whatever information the court may need to make decisions for your family. Their primary responsibility is to safeguard the interests of the children, and they will therefore be concerned with anything that may affect children. They should focus on finding out how children feel, and what they would like to happen (referred to as their 'wishes and feelings'). This should obviously be limited by the children's age and maturity, and many other factors. Depending on the circumstances, the court may ask them to investigate specific areas as diverse as accommodation for children, or allegations of domestic abuse.

You should be given information about Cafcass, what the officer will do, how to complain, etc. Make sure you take this in: it's easy to overlook when snowed under with other paperwork. You can also get a copy of their practice guidelines, which give more detailed information (Cafcass website: Part Four, No 31).

Practice still varies depending on where you live. Each service has evolved according to local needs, e.g. a large urban service will be different to one serving a less densely populated rural area. It is also acknowledged that individual officers have different approaches to their work, and despite improvements, have wide discretion to work as they choose. All this makes it almost impossible to predict what to expect.

They may meet you and your ex-partner together and/or separately, with your children or not. They may visit your home, or ask you to their office. It is possible to ask the officer how he or she will carry out the investigation, e.g. try to make sure that the children are seen with *both* parents. Cafcass has extensive powers to get information about you and your children from many sources, although they should inform you about this. You should also be kept informed about what Cafcass is likely to recommend. The report written for the court may not always reflect what you are expecting, even if you have been kept up to date.

After conducting the investigation into your circumstances, the Cafcass officer will write the report. This usually contains recommendations for what they consider will be the best outcome for the children. The recommendations are usually (but not always) followed, unless there are other reasons not to do so. The officer should keep you informed about the substance of the report and you or your representative should be told when the report has been submitted to the court and of your right to a copy. *Make sure you get this as early as possible.* If you are not satisfied with the accuracy of information or the opinions on which recommendations will be made, you will need time to try to get this changed. It is much more difficult to correct or query anything in the report once you get to the court. You can request that the officer attends court to answer any questions you may have.

From the Cafcass website:

> "It is very important that you do tell the court if you are unhappy with anything in the report, as it is harder to put it right later once the court proceedings are finished."

If you are unhappy with the service you have received from Cafcass, you can make a complaint. If you haven't been given details of their complaints procedure, look on their website (Part Four, No 31). Making a complaint about how the investigation into your family case was conducted after a court order has been made will not change the judgement.

Cafcass may also provide funding for mediation services outside the court and works closely with some contact centres, and other family support services. They are also now employing in-house Family Support Workers. Another promising development is the increasing use of Family Group Conferences (FGCs). These provide opportunities for the whole family (including children and/or their advocate), to come together to focus on the needs of the children, and to make their own family plan to share support and care. If Cafcass becomes involved in your arrangements for children, it's worth asking if they can offer you a Family Group Conference. It can be a very positive, forgiving day, as this grandmother said to a conference coordinator:

"We couldn't have organised this kind of day ourselves. Thank you for explaining how important it was for us all to talk to each other, even when at first, we really resisted

being in the same room. I cried when I found out they really do want me to be part of her (grandchild's) life…I thought they wanted to cut me out. So many misunderstandings…"

In a nutshell, the work that Cafcass does, either itself or via other services, is central to the family justice system. Their website includes lots of information for children and parents, plus their national guidelines, annual reports, business plans, and complaints procedure. Feedback is also now encouraged via online surveys, and children are able to email their questions and comments.

You are advised to remember that Cafcass has considerable influence over much that happens within the court. The FNF guide to Cafcass (p118) is essential reading and also gives advice on how to conduct yourself when in contact with this service. Failing to make a good impression could seriously affect the outcome for your family.

Local FNF meetings are also a good source of practical advice, from parents who have already been 'through the system'.

"Advice received from previous (FNF) meetings has helped me remain calm when Cafcass became involved. I believe this will contribute to a good outcome for my young daughter who is saying that she doesn't want to see me.

"Had I not listened to everyone's advice, the meeting with Cafcass would certainly have got my back up. Being human I would probably have answered back – it is difficult to accept allegations of bad parenting from someone who does not know you or how you interact with your child. I didn't express any negative opinions or judgements against the other parent, just left the officer to come to her own conclusions.

"I am very relieved to say that the Cafcass officer has suggested that I could apply for a Shared Residence Order as she believes my daughter is being alienated by the other parent. The officer said she would support me in the application."

Develop a good working relationship with your officer if at all possible. Although individual FNF members' experiences of Cafcass are still mixed, the number of good reports is increasing. It is encouraging to hear of instances where Cafcass worked in a non-judgemental way to ensure that children get the best of both parents' worlds. One father said that he was able to ring his officer when something unexpected happened between court hearings. Not only was she able to offer practical advice, but also intervened to help move things forward for the sake of his child.

As said earlier, Cafcass are now acknowledging that children should benefit from both parents and their two homes:

"Children should feel that they have a home with both parents, regardless of the amount of time they spend with them."
(*Handbook on the Parenting Course for Separating Parents*: Part 1, p27, Cafcass: Part Four, No 69).

How swiftly this will be reflected in the practices of individual officers, at local levels, remains to be seen. Past experience has shown that the personal 'opinions' (and it must be said, prejudices), of some officers can override any such guidance, limiting more balanced and supportive parenting outcomes for children.

We can only hope that as this service continues to evolve, it will eventually be able to consistently provide the support our separated families have needed for many years.

Using 'the system'

If you have to use the family justice system to find a solution for your family, be warned that there is no certainty of outcome, and many are deeply disappointed, even shocked by judgements made. Being told by a judge that you cannot see your own children is hard to swallow. But the decisions made in family proceedings are not necessarily final, and you may be successful on appeal. Failing that, it will normally be possible to try again later, especially if circumstances change.

As you seek help, bear in mind that those working in the system are just doing a job. They will only have a brief involvement with your family. When they have played their part, their interest is over. You and yours however, will have to live with the outcome. Therefore don't expect too much, have a realistic idea about what can be done, whether solutions can be found. Get as much information as you can, and don't rely on miracles.

One of the biggest difficulties when trying to describe 'the system' is that there are so many variables to take into account. This makes the outcome or likely judgement unpredictable. It is widely recognised that views and approaches vary considerably even within each profession or service that you may need to work with.

If you are unfortunate enough to have to become involved in legal action, this means that the outcome of your case will be different depending on which people are involved on the case, which judge is in court on the day. Practices also vary depending on where your case is heard. It is therefore vital to get local feedback, before risking the future of your family on this lottery.

"Quite a number of the fathers who come to branch meetings have been so confused by the advice they have had, that they start to think not about what they actually want and instead are concerned only about what they might get. I find it helps them if they are simply asked, 'What do you actually want so far as the children are concerned?' When they formulate an answer to this, I have not heard one single father say anything absurd or unreasonable, nor even completely unattainable. But by not having the answer clearly in their minds from the start, they often become intimidated and wracked with guilt about possibly upsetting the children by asking to see them, or for shared residence."

It is so easy to be 'outmanoeuvred' by the system. If you are well informed, and know what you want, you have a better chance of achieving a positive outcome for your family.

SUMMARY: FOR THE SAKE OF THE CHILDREN

To sum up some of the main points raised by this guide, finding out what you need to know is just a start. Coming to terms with life after divorce or separation means making difficult choices, sometimes with limited options. No one is prepared for what happens when families split up. It can come as quite a shock if you find you are outside your children's lives. Continuing to be a responsible parent may not be as straightforward as you had imagined.

"Fathers are so important."

The positive contribution that fathers make to their children's lives is now more widely acknowledged. There are major initiatives to raise awareness of this valuable role, and to encourage father involvement. But be aware that you may not find the same support for your continuing involvement after your family splits up. In fact, what you may find is a complete reversal of attitudes. For example, if the other parent stops your children seeing you, and you subsequently take legal action, your determination not to be cut out of the parenting picture may be misinterpreted.

"Why don't they just give up? If I was in a similar position I would."

To get this in perspective, would anyone advise a father *inside* a family to give up? Nevertheless, once you are relegated to (or accept) second parenting place, attitudes do change, and many may not make sufficient effort to include you. This applies not only to attitudes within 'the system'. The other parent is the key to what happens next. Your continuing relationship with your children largely depends on their agreement and co-operation. If for whatever reason they do not want to encourage this relationship, it will not be easy for any of you.

Throughout the guide, you have been advised to act as positively and reasonably as you can, and to explore all available avenues to reach an amicable and workable solution yourselves. You have been encouraged to try to get some dialogue going, to try to explain what's happening to the children.

However, this advice has often been followed by *'If this is not possible in your case...'*

The fathers (and mothers) who have fed into this project have direct experience of the reality of resistance to their continued parenting. They are more than willing to enter into whatever negotiations may be necessary for their children. *The main stumbling block may be that no one else seems to want or need to talk to them.* And they are effectively powerless if the other parent decides to exclude them.

"I'm his mother. I don't **have** to ask."

Undoubtedly after family breakdown, children are routinely losing contact with one parent usually (but not always) their fathers. Can it really be best for them if they 'lose' or in the worst cases, actively reject half their family support network? There needs to be a radical re-think of what causes conflict after parents split up. Giving one unreasonable parent almost total control causes a power imbalance that is impossible to negotiate.

> "It is time to concentrate on behaviour that damages children, ask what is preventing their continuing contact with this wider support network, rather than advising the non-abusing parent to 'back-off'. Many countries are accepting the importance of more equal sharing of parental responsibility and care after family breakdown. Policies and practices concerned with children and family breakdown must reinforce the benefits of enabling children to know and be loved by their 'whole' family."

Government consultations during the past ten or so years seem to acknowledge the need for change, and some progress has been made. Significantly, the Children and Adoption Act 2006 gives the courts more flexible powers to make sure children have a relationship with both their families.

Will this result in better outcomes for children, and will implacable hostility at last be dealt with more robustly? Only time will tell. But these essential changes are underway, sending a clear message that indeed both parents do matter. You will hopefully be even more determined to share more fully in your children's upbringing, and to *'draw a line in the sand'* when you feel that what is happening to your children is damaging, or what is asked of you or them cannot be justified.

"Yesterday I went to court for my final hearing. Cafcass was involved giving their recommendations. I got what Cafcass said I should have. Before yesterday I was only seeing my daughter three nights per month. Now I have a shared residency order and have my daughter for over night visits two nights each week and every other weekend. I feel this is a great result for her. Can you pass this message on to other fathers who are in my position "

"Never give up hope."

PUT YOURSELF IN YOUR CHILDREN'S SHOES

Children have needs and problems that are separate from those of their parents. Can you put yourself in their shoes?

We have argued that throughout the stressful and uncertain journey of separation, *either* parent can become so focused on their own problems that they lose sight of the fact that children are also trying to make sense of what's happening. Even with the best intentions, decisions can be made for them, but they may not be what children want or need...especially if no one attempts to include them in discussions.

Children, even young children, should be involved in decisions that affect their lives. NB: that is not the same as giving them the burden of responsibility to make these decisions themselves. As they mature, they should begin to appreciate the logistical constraints upon making arrangements (e.g. work schedules of parents, distance between homes, cost and time implications of moving between homes). Without this maturity, they will have unreasonable expectations of what can be practically achieved, despite the focus on their best interests. But they still need to know about changes that will impact upon them.

In the information section you will find a reference to *Dinosaurs Divorce – A Guide for Changing Families* (Part Four, No 60). This colourful book, published in the USA (and conspicuously more even-handed and non-judgemental than the UK about shared care post-separation), covers many of the problems and fears children might face when their parents separate. It also gives them ideas on how to take control of uncomfortable or unfamiliar situations.

> "*Dinosaurs Divorce* is a great book to snuggle up and read with young children going through divorce. Even older siblings seem interested in reading it. It helps children understand the feelings they may have while going through the divorce, learn how to handle mistakes parents sometimes make, and deal in a positive way with their changing family and living arrangement. The most important thing children learn from this book is that their parents' love for them will never change."
>
> (Book review: Amazon.co.uk)

Although the book is aimed at children, it could also help *both* parents to see things from a child's perspective. All too often, policy (e.g. CMEC) and practice works from the premise that the behaviour of only one parent needs addressing.

In reality, either parent can fail to grasp the impact that their behaviour is having upon their children. For example, learning from the examples set for them, children might be drawn into the manipulation of one parent by the other, or begin to believe one parent doesn't care about them.

The unique circumstances of each separated family present different challenges for parents – mums and dads.

If care is shared, both parents will be apart from their children for some of the time, and both will have to deal with this loss of 'being there' for them. And the transfer of children from one parent to the other gives the main opportunity to air concerns, real or imagined, often in front of children.

But many parents will be apart from their children for long spans of time. Some may be relatively powerless to fully engage with their children's lives on a regular (or indeed any) basis, however much they care, however much they seek to do so.

So, acknowledging the wide spectrum of family situations upon separation, the following 'food for thought' is based on issues highlighted in *Dinosaurs Divorce*, raising awareness of the potential problems and uncertainties children may be experiencing.

Not all the questions will be appropriate for every situation. But if you are fortunate to be able to spend time with your children, and where possible, even if you are at a distance from your children...imagine yourself in their shoes...

Food for thought

Take your time to think about each question. They are for *both* parents, *because all parents make mistakes.*

Those working with families throughout separation may also find the questions help to focus on behaviour (of either parent) that might not be putting children first.

> *Research into verbal and nonverbal communication shows that tone of voice (38%) and body language (55%) play major roles in how and what we communicate. Spoken words account for just 7%*
> *(Prof Mehrabian: Part Four, No 83).*

> *What is your behaviour saying to your children?*
> *What is their behaviour saying to you?*

Do you talk to them about the changes to their lives...even if you think they may be too young to understand?

Are they able to talk to you about how their lives might change?

*Do you **listen** to them? **Really** listen...?*

~ ~ ~

Are your children confused by change?

Do you understand why?

How can you best help them to manage change?

Are you a 'glass half empty' or a 'glass half full' parent?

What do they learn from you?

~ ~ ~

Do you reassure them that both parents still love them?

Do you show you value the contribution the other parent makes?

Are you willing to protect your child from any negative feelings and complaints you might have about the other parent?

Do you (ever) argue where your children can hear?

Are you always aware that they might be listening?

~ ~ ~

Do you encourage your child to love their other parent?

Or do they feel guilty because they love their other parent?

Do your children feel sad for you when they are with their other parent?

~ ~ ~

Do you show respect for the time when the other parent is on-duty?[1]

Are your children clear about when each parent will be on-duty?

Do you accept the differences in the other parent's style of parenting?

~ ~ ~

Who makes the decisions when changes to their schedule need to be made?

How do you feel when your children want to change arrangements, e.g. to spend time with their friends?

---

1   'On-duty' is a practical term used by Bannock County Court, Idaho, USA (Part Four, No 72).

How do they feel if you get grumpy?

If you and/or the other parent find new partners, how does your child feel?

Do new partners understand these feelings?

~ ~ ~

What role in the life of your child can a new partner play?

What role would your child want them/not want them to play?

Does everyone give children time to adjust?

~ ~ ~

How do your children feel about sharing with stepchildren or half-siblings?

Do you encourage them to share their feelings with you?

~ ~ ~

Do your children know that no matter what, they are still special?

As said at the beginning of this section, children have needs (and wishes and feelings) that may be very different to your own. Like you and their other parent, they need time, understanding and support to make sense of major family changes.

No matter what you are having to cope with, make space to ask yourself: "If I were in my child's shoes, how would I feel, and what would I need from my parents?"

Finally, in terms of never giving up hope, here are some constructive strategies from an enlightened family court in Arizona, USA:

It's never too late to...

> *Fix things if they're broken. Make plans. Don't give up. Schedule counseling. Take a parenting class. Have some fun.*

> *Make another effort to communicate with the other parent. Keep trying. Learn to communicate without "pushing buttons".*

> *Apologise to your children if you know you have hurt them with your behaviour or words. Keep them out of the middle. They will love you for it.*

> *Redirect unresolved anger by finding appropriate resources. You will feel better, and deserve it. So do your kids.*

➢   *Find constructive alternatives for problem-solving. Take charge. Surprise yourself!*

➢   *Forgive your former partner, and forgive yourself. Someone wise once said:*

"Forgiveness is a gift you give to yourself."
(An extract from 'Family Ties and Knots', Kat Cooper, USA: Part Four, No 64)

PART FOUR: Reference section

FAMILIES NEED FATHERS

'Keeping Children and Parents in Contact since 1974.'
Reg Charity No 276899

FNF welcomes membership enquiries. Anyone concerned about children losing contact with their families is encouraged to become a member.

> **Address**: 134 Curtain Road, London EC2A 3AR
> **Telephone**: 020 7613 5060
> **Email**: fnf@fnf.org.uk

www.fnf.org.uk: the FNF website is the most comprehensive starting point for up-to-date information, with links to every site you could possibly need. You can also join FNF on-line. There are additional pages for 'member only' access.

www.separatedfamiliesmatter.org.uk: an FNF website for those working with separated families.

The Families Need Fathers' National Telephone Helpline: run by trained volunteers who help many thousands of parents every year, usually as their first point of contact.

FNF local meetings: an opportunity to meet others who are experiencing similar family situations.

FNF Self-Help and FNF Chat: members' only Internet discussion forums – 'virtual' meetings, where problems, advice, information and strategies can be shared with other members.

FNF Publications (please enquire for current price list – discounts for FNF members):

Factsheets:

The Children Act 1989
Parental Responsibility
Interim Contact
Change of Surname
Representing Yourself
McKenzie Friends
Contact Guidelines
Locating Your Child
Grandparents
Effective Letter Writing
Child Support Agency & Child
    Maintenance Enforcement
    Commission
Family Mediation
Shared Residence
The Case for Shared Parenting - arguing
    for your children
Human Rights Act 1998
Parental Alienation

Booklets:

How to get the best Cafcass report for
your children and yourself
Guide to the Scots Legal System
The Presumption of Shared Residence
Schools and Parents
Parental Alienation
International Child Abduction
Preparing Court Bundles
The Judicial Complaints Process
Choosing & Using a Solicitor

Special report:
Giving Meaning to Psychological
    Research on Fathering
    (Sheila Rossan PhD Senior Lecturer
    Brunel University)

Guides:
What is Shared Parenting?
FNF Case for Shared Parenting in Social
    Policy
Finding Your Father

Books:
Give 'Em Some LIP! – A handbook for
    those using the family courts without
    a solicitor.

OTHER SOURCES OF ADVICE OR INFORMATION

(Be aware that this information may change, especially the contact details. Readers must assess the value of the information in the following sources of information and further reading. Neither FNF nor the author can accept any liability for any errors or omissions.)

1 **Action for Children**: excellent website for children.
   www.itsnotyourfault.org

2 **ADRnow: exploring alternatives to court**. The website gives an overview of ADR (alternative dispute resolution) schemes in the UK, an outline of how they work, and their pros and cons. It is independent of ADR providers and government.
   www.adrnow.org.uk

3 **The Advisory Centre for Education**: offers free, independent advice to families on all aspects of state-funded education for children of school age, including school exclusions, admissions and appeals, bullying and complaints. Useful publication: Making a complaint. A practical guide to parents' legal rights, 2007. General Advice: 0808 800 5793 (10 a.m. – 5 p.m. Mon-Fri).
   www.ace-ed.org.uk

4 **Advisory, Conciliation and Arbitration Service (ACAS)**: call 0845 747 4747 for maternity and paternity rights, entitlements and booklets
   www.acas.org.uk

5 **AIRE Centre (Advice on Individual Rights in Europe)**: can advise on the Human Rights Act and its impact on UK law. Advice Line: 020 7831 3850 (Tues and Thurs 2 p.m. – 5 p.m.).
   www.airecentre.org

6 **British and Irish Legal Information Institute (BAILII)**: find British and Irish case law & legislation, European Union case law, Law Commission reports, and other law-related British and Irish material.
   www.bailii.org

7   **British Telecom (BT)**: use 141 to withhold your number on a call-by-call basis. Simply dial '141' before making a call.

8   **Citizens Advice Bureau (CAB)**: a good starting point for advice on a wide range of issues affecting families. Lots of related literature and 'where to go next' information. Can refer to other organisations, including local services. Local phone numbers.
     www.adviceguide.org.uk

9   **Community Legal Advice (CLA)**: information on Legal Aid. Helpline 0845 345 4345. Legal Aid Calculator on website.
     www.communitylegaladvice.org.uk

10   *Family Law*: monthly journal available at main libraries. Lots of relevant information and latest family 'cases'. Includes articles written by judges and lawyers. Also, on the Internet, has a free Family Law update service, containing summaries of cases, legislation and practice developments (1997 onwards).
     www.familylaw.co.uk

11   **Family Mediators Association**: National Family Mediation Helpline Freephone 0808 200 0033
     www.thefma.co.uk

12   **Family Rights Group:** advice and support for families whose children are involved with social services. Founded by social workers, lawyers and families in 1974 in response to the injustices experienced by many families involved with social services and the unnecessary separation of children from their families. Free confidential advice service: 0800 731 1696 (Mon-Fri 10 a.m. –12 a.m., 1.30 p.m. – 3.30 p.m.).
     www.frg.org.uk

13   **Fatherhood Institute:** research and information on all aspects of fatherhood, for parents, policymakers and family workers.
     www.fatherhoodinstitute.org

14   **General Medical Council:** good practice guidance for all doctors working with children and young people from 0 –18 years.
     www.gmc-uk.org/guidance/archive/GMC_0-18.pdf

15   **Gingerbread/One Parent Families:** support and advice for lone parents, including fathers. Gingerbread has support groups for lone parent families throughout England and Wales. Each local branch is different, so worth investigating. Can help with welfare advice, childcare issues. For advice and information Freephone: 0800 018 5026 (Mon-Fri 9 a.m. – 5 p.m., Weds 9 a.m. – 8 p.m.).
www.gingerbread.org.uk

16   **Grandparents' Association**: support and information for all grandparents, including free factsheets for grandparents apart from children. Can also advise when there is social services involvement. Helpline: 0845 4349585
www.grandparents-association.org.uk

17   **JUMP (Jewish Unity for Mulitple Parenting)**: campaigning for improved relationships between divorced parents and their children, in the Jewish community, as well as nationally and internationally. Website includes a Jewish Parenting Plan.
www.jump-parenting.org.uk

18   **Mothers Apart from Their Children (MATCH):** deals with similar set of problems to FNF, but where the mother is the 'non resident' parent. BM Box 6334, London WC1N 3XX.
www.matchmothers.org.uk

19   **National Association of Child Contact Centres (NACCC):** can provide literature that can help you come to terms with the aims of centres and reassure re outcomes for children. Also has literature to help children (No 57 below). 0845 4500 280. Website has search for local centres.
www.naccc.org.uk

20   **National Association of Child Support Action (NACSA):** up-to-date Advice and information on the CSA plus a Helpline (subscription needed). NACSA, PO Box 4454, Dudley, West Midlands, DY1 9AN. Tel: 01384 572525
www.nacsa.org

21   **National Family Mediation (NFM):** 01392 271610 or in local phone book.
www.nfm.org.uk

22   **Parentline Plus:** offers support to anyone looking after a child. Free, confidential Helpline: 0808 800 2222.
www.parentlineplus.org.uk

23   **Relate (National Office):** offers a range of services for parents who are divorcing or separating, including counselling for children. Tel. 0300 100 1234 for details of local services.
www.relate.org.uk

24   **Resolution:** members are family solicitors with a Code of Practice that promotes an approach to family law that is sensitive, constructive, and non-confrontational. Website also includes an Advice Centre.
www.resolution.org.uk

25   **Reunite (National Council for Abducted Children):** adviceline 01162 556 234
www.reunite.org

26   **Shared Parenting Information Group (SPIG):** collates and promotes research information on shared parenting.
www.spig.clara.net

27   **Trades Union Congress (TUC):** information on employment rights and responsibilities, including maternity and paternity leave and pay and flexible working. Booklets available to read or download online. Know Your Rights Line: 0870 600 4882
www.tuc.org.uk

28   **UK College of Family Mediators:** 0117 904 7223. Website includes search facility for local services
www.ukcf.co.uk

29   **UNICEF (United Nations Children's Fund):** works throughout the world (190 countries) to protect and secure the rights of children. Upholds the Convention on the Rights of the Child.
www.unicef.org/crc

30   **Working Families:** a charity focusing on balancing employment and family life. Free legal Helpline for low income families 0800 013 0313
www.workingfamilies.org.uk

GOVERNMENT DEPARTMENTS

(INC USEFUL PUBLICATIONS)

Links to general government sites including those below, plus brief description can be found at: **www.direct.gov.uk**.

31   **Children and Family Court Advisory Support Service (Cafcass).**
      www.cafcass.gov.uk

32   **Children's Information Service (CIS)**: Councils (local and county) provide a wide range of community services; may include toy libraries, play buses. Also information on nurseries, crèches, authorised child-minders. 0800 234 6346, or via ChildcareLink 0800 096 02 96.
      www.childcarelink.gov.uk

33   **Community Legal Advice:** a free, confidential and impartial advice service paid for by legal aid (England & Wales only). Helpline 0845 345 4345 (Mon – Fri 9 a.m. – 6:30 p.m.). Website includes a legal aid calculator.
      www.communitylegaladvice.org.uk

34   **Community Legal Service (CLS)**: a network of organisations designed to make it easier for the public to get legal help and advice (England & Wales only). Also funds legal aid. Wide range of legal information on website.
      www.legalservices.gov.uk

35   **Child Maintenance Enforcement Commission (CMEC)**: find out about your options for making maintenance arrangements best suited to your circumstances 0800 988 0988. Website includes a form that could be used to record a privately agreed plan for children.
      www.cmoptions.org

36   **Child Support Agency (CSA):** national enquiry line: 08457 133133 – answers basic questions, plus CSA literature can be ordered. Comprehensive website.
      www.csa.gov.uk

37   **Department for Business Enterprise & Regulatory Reform (BERR):**
      information on rights to time off for family emergencies. Website guides
      include 'Time off for dependants: a guide to employers and employees',
      and 'Parental leave: A guide for employers and employees'.
      www.berr.gov.uk/employment/employment-legislation

38   **Department for Children, Schools and Families (DCSF):**
      www.dcsf.gov.uk

39   **Department of Health (DoH):** encompasses Social Services.
      www.dh.gov.uk

40   **The 10 Downing Street website:** ask the Prime Minister a question, plus
      e-petitions and responses.
      www.number10.gov.uk/communicate

41   **Department of Trade and Industry (DTI):** information for working parents.
      www.direct.gov.uk/employees

42   **General Record Office:** information about obtaining, or adding names to
      birth certificates.
      www.gro.gov.uk/gro/content/births

43   **HM Court Service (HMCS):** all the Children Act application forms you
      are ever likely to need can now be downloaded from their website in pdf
      format. The forms should also be available from your local court. Site
      includes a searchable database for local court contact details.

      Also includes the President's Guidance on McKenzie friends (14th April
      2008), and Leaflet EX710: 'Guidance on disclosing information about Family
      Proceedings involving children which are heard in private' (for court users
      and people receiving information).
      www.hmcourts-service.gov.uk

44   **HM Revenue and Customs (HMRC):** Children's Tax Credit Helpline: 0845
      300 3900.
      www.hmrc.gov.uk/taxcredits

45   **International Child Abduction and Contact Unit (ICACU)**: Hague
      Convention on the Civil Aspects of International Child Abduction (the
      Abduction Convention) 020 7911 7127
      www.courtfunds.gov.uk/os/icacu.htm

46   **Ministry of Justice**: the UK Statute Law Database (online) is the official
      revised edition of the primary legislation of the United Kingdom made
      available online. Includes the Children Act 1989 plus subsequent changes
      (updating is in progress: goes up to 2006 at the date of publication of
      this book).
      www.statutelaw.gov.uk

47   **Office for National Statistics**: includes reports related to children and
      families.
      www.statistics.gov.uk

48   **Office for Standards in Education, Children's Services and Skills (Ofsted)**:
      inspects and regulates care for children and young people (including Cafcass
      services), and inspects education and training for learners of all ages.
      www.ofsted.gov.uk

49   **The Ombudsman**: deals with complaints about government services.
      www.ombudsman.org.uk

50   **Office of Public Sector Information (OPSI):** website has up-to-date public
      sector information and legislation, including the 'Children and Adoption
      Act 2006', Chapter 20 – includes 'contact' activities and monitoring,
      enforcement orders, compensation for financial loss, family assistance orders.
      www.opsi.gov.uk/acts/acts2006/ukpga_20060020_en_1

51   **The Passport Office:** 0870 521 0410
      www.ips.gov.uk

52   **SureStart:** a government programme. Find information about local
      Children's Centres and childcare (also see No 73 below).
      www.surestart.gov.uk

FURTHER READING

(More books on FNF's website. NB: the charity gets five per cent of your total order anytime you buy books and other items from Amazon via FNF's website links.)

53   *A Practical Guide to Family Proceedings,* R H L Blomfield & Helen Brooks, (2008), Jordan Publishing.

54   *Children Act Handbook*, Herschman & McFarlane (2008/09), Jordan Publishing. Updated annually, a consolidated version of the Children Act 1989.

55   *Children Act Private Law Proceedings: A Handbook*, District Judge John Mitchell, 2nd revised edition (2006), Jordan Publishing.

56   *Absent Fathers?* Jonathan Bradshaw, Carol Stimson, Christine Skinner & Julie Williams (1999), Routledge.

57   *Ben's Story and Lily's Story,* two storybooks to introduce primary and nursery age children to Child Contact Centres, Linda Wyon, available from NACCC: 0845 4500 280.

58   *The Child Support Handbook* (updated regularly), Child Poverty Action Group.
020 7837 7979, or order online.
www.cpag.org.uk/publications/childsupport

59   *Dad's Place: A New Guide for Fathers After Divorce*, Jill Burrett (1996), Ward Lock.

60   *Dinosaurs Divorce: A Guide for Changing Families,* Marc Brown and Laurie Krasny Brown (1988), Little, Brown and Company. Brilliant for children *and* adults.

61   *Divorce Poison*, Dr Richard A Warshak (2002), Regan Books (available from Amazon via FNF's website link). Includes advice on how to counteract alienation.

62 **Enforcing the Gender Equality Duty: A Toolkit for Individuals**, Equalities and Human Rights Commission.
www.equalityhumanrights.com

63 **Family Law Protocol**, the Law Society with Resolution, Legal Services Commission and the Department for Constitutional Affairs (2nd edition 2006), The Law Society.

64 **Family Ties and Knots**, Kat Cooper, Superior Court's Office, Family Court Services, Maricopa County, Arizona, USA. Thought-provoking booklet aimed at both parents. Website includes a video.
www.familytiesandknots.com

65 **Fathercare**, John Griffiths (1997), Colt Books.

66 **Fatherneed: Why Father Care is as Essential as Mother Care for Your Child**, Kyle D Pruett (2000), Free Press.

67 **Fatherhood Reclaimed**, Adrienne Burgess (1998), Vermillion.

68 **Getting to Yes**, Roger Fisher (2nd expanded edition 1997), Arrow Books.

69 **Handbook on the Parenting Course for Separating Parents: Parts 1 & 2,** Cafcass (2009). Only available to download from the Cafcass website.
www.cafcass.gov.uk/publications/leaflets_for_adults.aspx

70 **How to Make an Application in the Family Proceedings Court**, Paul Mallender & Jane Rayson (1992), Blackstone Press.

71 **Kids in the Middle: An Agony Aunt's Guide for Parting Parents and Their Children**, Deidre Sanders (2008), DCSF.

72 **Long Distance Parenting**, Bannock County Court, Idaho, USA. Ideas to reassure your child you are still there, when apart from them.
www.bannockcounty.us/courts/divorce/dmoretip.htm

73 **Looking for Childcare? A SureStart Guide to Help You Make the Right Choices**, SureStart (2007), DCSF. A guide to childcare and early education

choices for parents. Covers financial support, health, learning development and flexible working. Available from DCSF Publications service, ref 00332-2007BKT-EN. 0845 60 222 60, or download from website. **www.surestart.gov.uk/aboutsurestart/parents/lookingforchildcare**

74   *Lost Children: A Guide for Separating Parents,* Penny Cross (2000), Velvet Glove Publishing: 01959 577079.

75   *A Man's Place in the Home: Fathers and Families in the UK*, Charlie Lewis (2000), Joseph Rowntree Foundation.

76   *My Family's Changing*, Cafcass *(2008)*. Two booklets for children (under and over 12s).
     www.cafcass.gov.uk/ publications.aspx

77   *National Family Mediation Guide to Separation and Divorce: The Complete Handbook for Managing a Fair and Amicable Divorce*, Thelma Fisher (1997), Vermillion.

78   *Outrageous Fortune*, Terence Frisby (1998), First Thing Publications.

79   *Parenting Plans – Putting Children First: A Guide for Separating Parents*, DCSF (2008), the Stationery Office, or pdf on Cafcass website.
     www.tso.co.uk or www.cafcass.gov.uk

80   *Parenting Threads: Caring for Children When Couples Part,* Erica De'Ath (1992), National Stepfamily Association.

81   *Planning for Shared Parenting: A Guide for Parents Living Apart*, sponsored by the Massachusetts Chapter of the Association of Family and Conciliation Courts (AFCC), USA. Includes rationale for sharing care at different ages and stages of children's development.
     www.hampshireprobate.com/parentprogram/sharedparenting.pdf

82   *Schools, 'Parents' and 'Parental Responsibility'*, DCSF.
     www.teachernet.gov.uk/management/atoz/p/parentalresponsibility

83 **Silent Messages: A Wealth of Information About Nonverbal Communication** (body language), A Mehrabian (1981).
www.kaaj.com/psych

84 **Time For Children**, Cafcass (2008).
www.cafcass.gov.uk/ publications.aspx

85 **What the Family Courts Expect from Parents,** Midland Region Family Judges and Magistrates (2009). An even-handed leaflet for separating parents, that hopefully will be available in all family courts.
www.hmcourts-service.gov.uk/cms/files/family_final.pdf

86 **Why Are My Parents Separating?** Diane Louise Jordan (2000), from the 'Coping With Growing' Audio Series, Backbone Productions Ltd.
www.copingwithgrowing.com

AND FINALLY

If you have found this book useful, help us to make future editions even better. Attitudes and practices in legal and social policy are rapidly changing. Your experiences can help others – make sure we hear about them. Write or email to:

The Editor
'For the Sake of the Children'
FNF National Office
134 Curtain Road, London EC2A 3AR
Email: fnf@fnf.org.uk

Index

Notes

Notes